The Encyclopedia of
North American Indians

Volume IV

Deloria, Ella – General Allotment Act

General Editor
D. L. Birchfield

Marshall Cavendish

DELORIA, ELLA (1888–1971)

Ella Cara Deloria, who was also known as Anpetu Waste Win, was born in the White Swan District of the Yankton Sioux Reservation. Her father was an Episcopal minister who established a mission on the Lakota Standing Rock Reservation, and her mother was a member of the Yankton Sioux. Deloria's father was of French ancestry, and she learned English and the Nakota dialect of the Sioux language fluently.

She is the aunt of well-known Native American author Vine Deloria, Jr. Because she was raised by Christian parents of both European and French ancestry, much of Ella Deloria's writing deals with the problems and struggles of individuals living in a world of competing cultures.

Deloria attended the All Saints Boarding School in Sioux Falls, South Dakota, Oberlin College in Ohio, and Columbia University in New York City, where she received a Bachelor of Science degree in 1915. At Columbia, she worked with anthropologist Franz Boas translating a series of Lakota Sioux stories by George Bushotter. She taught at All Saints Boarding School from 1914 to 1916 and at the Haskell Institute in Lawrence, Kansas, in 1923.

In 1927, Deloria resumed work with Boas on a project concerning Lakota traditional stories. She became frustrated with the project, however, when she was unable to document the authenticity of a collection of stories compiled by James Walker (now available in a publication entitled *Lakota Myth*, 1983). Deloria also worked with Boas on a work entitled *Dakota Grammar*, a dictionary of the Dakota language. This was published as *Memoirs of the National Academy of Sciences*, vol. 23, no. 2 (1941).

Much of Deloria's work is unpublished, including "Dakota Autobiographies" (c. 1937) and "Dakota Speeches" (1937?). Her published work includes *Waterlily*, a fictional ethnography written in the 1940s but not published until 1988, and *Speaking of Indians* (1944), an essay concerning Sioux culture.

In her fictional narrative *Waterlily*, Deloria explores cultural confrontation by examining specific people and their human struggles. The story portrays the lives of Waterlily and her mother, Blue Bird, members of a Lakota family on the Dakota plains.

During Waterlily's birth, her mother is forced to come to terms with the competing demands of childbirth and Lakota ritual. As a young woman, Waterlily must make a decision to break certain ceremonial rules in order to help a young man. Lowanla, for whom Waterlily shows a youthful romantic interest, is performing the ritual ceremony of the Sun Dance. Waterlily is thoroughly familiar with the rules of the ceremony, which restrict her participation.

In a moment of extreme emotional conflict, in which the demands of Lakota ceremony and the demands of her heart are at odds, Waterlily decides to go against traditional rules and secretly brings Lowanla a forbidden drink of water. Waterlily must eventually choose between tribal loyalty and love.

Through the course of the story, Waterlily and her mother are presented with many such decisions. Through these decisions, Deloria illustrates the complexity of her characters' lives and natures. In showing understanding of and sympathy for the complexity of human experience, Deloria emphasizes the similarities that reach across cultural boundaries rather than differences.

Throughout her writing, Deloria describes a wide variety of relationships from both Native and European-American perspectives. Her multicultural heritage and her vigorous interest in Siouan tradition give her the ability and insight to explore these compelling issues of cultural conflict.

SEE ALSO:

Bushotter, George; Deloria, Vine, Jr.; Haskell Indian Nations University; Siouan Languages; Sioux Literature, Contemporary.

SUGGESTED READING:

Prater, John. "Ella Deloria: Varied Intercourse," *Wicazo Sa Review*, volume XI, number 2 (Fall 1995), pp. 40–46.

DELORIA, VINE, JR. (1933–)

Vine Deloria, Jr., was born on the Pine Ridge Reservation in South Dakota. A Standing Rock Sioux author, attorney, professor, and public speaker on Indian issues, he was educated at Iowa State University, the Lutheran School of Theology, and the University of Colorado Law School.

Deloria became active as a public speaker on Indian issues in the 1960s. He is a well-known author and has published such works as *Custer Died for Your Sins* (1969); *We Talk, You Listen: New Tribes, New Turf* (1970); *God Is Red* (1973); and, most recently, *Red Earth, White Lies: Native Americans and the Myth of Scientific Fact* (1995).

In the 1980s, Deloria supported his nation's efforts to try to regain the Black Hills, land that is sacred to the Sioux people. He was one who did not wish to see the people accept money from the federal government as a settlement for taking the sacred hills, which the Sioux call Paha Sapa. The Sioux were offered millions of dollars in compensation by the U.S. Claims Commission, but they have refused the money, insisting that the Black Hills must be returned to them.

Deloria has been the executive director of the National Congress of American Indians (NCAI). During his leadership of NCAI, the organization became increasingly critical of the United States government's Indian policies. He is also a university professor and continues to write books concerning Indian issues.

SEE ALSO:
Black Hills; Deloria, Ella; Siouan Nations.

DEMAIN, PAUL (1955–)

Paul DeMain, who is also known as Oshscabewis, is a journalist, business entrepreneur, and Native activist. Born in Milwaukee, he is a tribal citizen of the Wisconsin Oneida Nation and a descendant of the White Earth Ojibway (Chippewa) Band. He is the founder and chief executive officer of Indian Country Communications, Inc. (ICC), a privately owned Native-controlled business located on the Lac Courte Oreilles Chippewa reservation in northern Wisconsin. ICC is the publisher of *News from Indian Country*, a nationally and internationally circulated Native newspaper, and *Explore*

Indian Country, a monthly Native casino and entertainment magazine.

DeMain has also been the managing editor of *News from Indian Country* and *Explore Indian Country* from 1987 to the present. He was managing editor of the "LCO Journal," for WOJB-FM radio, in Hayward, Wisconsin, in 1987. He has served as president of the Native American Journalists' Association (NAJA), from 1992 to 1994, and has been a member of the NAJA Board of Directors from 1986 to 1987 and 1990 to 1994. He has also served as president of UNITY '94 Alliance, an international organization of journalists of color, including the National Associations of Black, Hispanic, Asian, and Native American Journalists, in 1994.

DeMain majored in journalism at the University of Wisconsin–Eau Claire from 1975 to 1977. In 1980, he was admitted to the Wisconsin Lac Courte Oreilles Tribal Bar Association. From 1987 to 1988, he served as American Indian educational counselor and recruiter for the University of Wisconsin–Eau Claire. He has served on many councils and advisory commissions, including the Wisconsin Governor's Interstate Indian Council Executive Board, 1986–1988, and the Wisconsin Governor's Council on Minority Business Development, 1983–1988. He has also served as the Wisconsin Governor's Advisor on Indian Affairs Policy, 1983–1987, and the Wisconsin Governor's representative on the State Council on Alcohol and Other Drug Abuse, 1983–1987.

In addition to his professional achievements, DeMain belongs to the Medicine Lodge Society and the Big Drum Societies at the Lac Courte Oreilles and Lac du Flambeau reservations. He is a grass dancer and a singer with the Lac Courte Oreilles Soldier's Drum and with the Lac Courte Oreilles Badger Singers. He also enjoys amateur archaeology as a hobby.

SEE ALSO:
Native American Journalists Association; Ojibwe.

DEMOGRAPHY, NATIVE

The question of the number of people who lived in the Americas prior to permanent contact with

Europeans has become the object of a lively demographic debate during the last third of the twentieth century. (The study of human populations and such factors as the size, growth, density, distribution, and ethnic or racial character of a population group is known as demography.) This debate involves two very different ways of looking at historical and archaeological evidence. One side in the population debate restricts itself to strict interpretation of the written evidence at hand. Another point of view accepts the probability that observers (usually of European ancestry) recorded only a fraction of the events that actually occurred in the Americas.

The fact that disease was the major cause of Native depopulation is not at issue here—both sides agree on the importance of disease in the depopulation of the Americas to the point where many settlers thought they had come to an empty land that was theirs for the taking. The debate is over the number of Native people who died. The plagues brought to the Americas by contact with non-Native people have not ended, even today. For example, between 1988 and 1990, 15 percent of the Yanomami of Brazil, who had only limited contact with people of European descent until this time, died of malaria, influenza, and even the common cold.

Henry F. Dobyns of the Newberry Library in Chicago estimates that about 16 million Native Americans lived in North America north of Mesoamerica, the area populated by the Aztecs and other Central American Native nations, at the time of Christopher Columbus's first voyage. Since population densities were much greater in Central America and along the Andes, an estimate of 16 million north of Mesoamerica indicates to Dobyns that 90 to 112 million Native people lived in all of the Americas before the year 1500, making some parts of the Western Hemisphere as densely populated at the time as many fertile areas of Europe and Asia.

This Diego Rivera mural at the National Palace in Mexico City depicts the arrival of Hernán Cortés at Veracruz on April 22, 1519. It offers ample evidence of the treatment that lay in store for the indigenous peoples of Mexico at the hands of the Spaniards.

Dobyns's estimates of indigenous population at contact represent a radical departure from earlier tallies. The first "systematic" count was compiled during the early twentieth century by James Mooney, who maintained that 1,153,000 people lived in the land area now occupied by the United States at the time of European contact. By contrast, Mooney calculated the 1907 Native population in the same area at 406,000. Dividing the country into regions, he calculated the percentage loss ranging from 61 percent (in the North Atlantic states) to 93 percent in California.

Following Mooney, the most widely followed population estimates were provided beginning in 1939 by A. L. Kroeber in his book *Cultural and Natural Areas of Native North America*. By Kroeber's determination, only about 900,000 Native people occupied North America north of Mexico at the time of European contact. According to Ann F. Ramenofsky, Kroeber did not consider disease as a factor in depopulation because he feared that such an emphasis would lead to an overestimation of precontact population sizes.

Defending his precontact population estimates, Dobyns argues that "absence of evidence does not mean absence of phenomenon," especially where written records are scanty, as in America before or just after permanent European contact. Dobyns maintains that European epidemic diseases invaded a relatively disease-free environment in the Americas with amazing rapidity, first in Mesoamerica (with the Spanish), arriving in eastern North America along Native trade routes long before English and French settlers arrived. The fact that the French explorer Jacques Cartier observed the deaths of fifty Natives in the village of Stadacona in 1535 indicates to Dobyns that many more may have died in other villages that Cartier never saw. Because of the lack of evidence, conclusions must be drawn from what little remains, according to Dobyns, who extends his ideas to other continents as well: "Lack of Chinese records of influenza does not necessarily mean that the Chinese did not suffer from influenza; an epidemic could have gone unrecorded, or records of it may not have survived," Dobyns has written.

Some critics of Dobyns claim that he has misused a few pieces of documented evidence in an effort to justify his claims that epidemics were widespread in the 1500s. To the critics of Dobyns, the fact that fifty Natives were recorded as dying at Stadacona means just that: fifty Natives died, no more, no fewer. To Dobyns, however, such arguments downplay the magnitude of Native American populations and their complex social structures at the time of European contact.

While Snow and Lanphear, of the State University of New York at Albany, maintain that "there were often buffer zones between population concentrations or isolates that would have impeded the spread of diseases," Dobyns replies that the practice of trade, war, diplomacy, and other demographic movements obliterated such "buffer zones," and aided the spread of disease. Snow and Lanphear also assert that the sparseness of Native populations in North America above the Rio Grande slowed the spread of disease, a point of view that does not account for the speed with which smallpox and other infections spread once they reached a particular area.

Dobyns not only denies that buffer zones existed but maintains that smallpox was only the most virulent of several diseases to devastate Native populations. The others, roughly in descending order of deadliness, included measles, influenza, bubonic plague, diphtheria, typhus, cholera, and scarlet fever. According to Dobyns, "The frontier of European/Euroamerican settlement in North America was not a zone of interaction between people of European background and vacant land, nor was it a region where initial farm colonization achieved any 'higher' use of the land as measured in human population density. It was actually an interethnic frontier of biological, social, and economic interchange between Native Americans and Europeans and/or Euroamericans." The most important point to Snow and Lanphear, however, is "where one puts the burden of proof in this argument, or, for that matter, in any argument of this kind. . . . We cannot allow ourselves to be tricked into assuming the burden of disproving assertions for which there is no evidence."

Given the evidence they have in hand, however, even Snow and Lanphear acknowledge that between two-thirds and 98 percent of the Native peoples inhabiting areas of the northeastern United States died in epidemics between roughly 1600 and 1650. The Western Abenakis, for example, declined from 12,000 to 250 (98 percent), the Massachusetts (including the Narragansett) from 44,000 to 6,400 (85 percent), the Mohawks from 8,100 to 2,000 (75 percent), and the Eastern Abenakis from 13,800 to 3,000 (78 percent).

David Henige of the University of Wisconsin–Madison also criticizes Dobyns for "remorseless attention to disease to the exclusion of all else," as the major cause of depopulation among Native peoples: "We might well ask why he does not consider the possible role of such factors as warfare, land exhaustion, climatic pressure, or cultural changes."

The range of population estimates at European contact reflects a diverse range of viewpoints on the role of disease and other factors. William M. Denevan, who edited a collection of articles surveying population estimates for 1492 across North and South America, arrived at a consensus figure of 53.9 million Native people for the entire Western Hemisphere, including 3.8 million north of Mesoamerica. These figures represent a small decline from his first set of estimates, made in 1976.

Creek poet Joy Harjo has observed that Native people were not meant to survive on this continent. This Grand Entry at a contemporary powwow competition is a testimony to the survival of Native culture against overwhelming odds.

Given the number of people killed and the lengthy period during which they have died, the world has probably not again seen such continuous human misery over such a large area. Tenochtitlán, the Aztecs' capital city (which occupied the site of present-day Mexico City) struck Hernán Cortés as a world-class metropolis when he first looked out over it in 1519. The Aztec metropolis is estimated to have contained 250,000 people at a time when Rome, Seville, and Paris housed about 150,000 each. Before he destroyed it, Cortés stared at the splendor of the Aztec capital and called Tenochtitlán the most beautiful city in the world.

Spanish chronicler Bernal Díaz del Castillo stood atop a great temple in Tenochtitlán and described causeways eight paces wide, teeming with thousands of people, crossing lakes and channels dotted by convoys of canoes. He said that Spanish soldiers who had been to Rome or Constantinople told Diaz that "for convenience, regularity and population, they have never seen the like."

Within a decade, epidemics of smallpox and other diseases carried by the conquistadores had killed at least half the Aztecs. One of the Aztec chroniclers who survived wrote, "Almost the whole population suffered from racking coughs and painful, burning sores." The plague that followed the Spanish conquest spread in roughly concentric circles from the islands of Hispaniola and Cuba to the mainland of present-day Mexico. Bartolomé de Las Casas, the Roman Catholic priest who criticized Spanish treatment of Native peoples, said that when the first visitors found it, Hispaniola (present-day Haiti and Dominican Republic) was a beehive of people. Within one lifetime, the forests were silent. Within thirty years of Cortés's arrival in Mexico, the Native population had fallen from about 25 million to roughly 6 million.

A century later, entering North America, the Puritans often wondered why the lands on which they settled, which otherwise seemed so bountiful, had been wiped clean of their Native inhabitants. Four years before the *Mayflower* landed, a plague of smallpox had swept through Native American villages along the coast of the area the settlers would rename as "New" England. John Winthrop admired abandoned Native cornfields and then declared that God had provided the epidemic that killed the people who had tended them as an act of divine providence.

"God," Winthrop said, "hath hereby cleared our title to this place." As settlement spread westward, Native people learned to fear the sight of the honeybee. These "English flies" usually colonized areas about 100 miles (160 kilometers) in advance of the frontier, and the first sight of them came to be regarded as a harbinger of death.

The virulence of the plagues from Europe may be difficult to comprehend in our time. Even in Europe, where immunities had developed to many of the most serious diseases, one in seven people died in typical smallpox epidemics. Half the children born in Europe at the time of contact never reached the age of fifteen. Life expectancy for people on both sides of the Atlantic averaged thirty-five years.

— B. E. Johansen

SEE ALSO:

Aztec; Caribbean, Indigenous Cultures of; Central America, Indigenous Peoples of; Columbian Exchange; Columbus, Christopher; Cortés, Hernán; Epidemic Diseases; Las Casas, Bartolomé de; Maya.

SUGGESTED READINGS:

Denevan, William M., ed. *The Native American Population of the Americas in 1492*. Madison: University of Wisconsin Press, 1976.

Dobyns, Henry F. *Their Numbers Become Thinned*. Knoxville: University of Tennessee Press, 1983.

Ramenofsky, Ann F. *Vectors of Death: The Archeology of European Contact*. Albuquerque: University of New Mexico Press, 1987.

Wright, Ronald. *Stolen Continents: The Americas Through Indian Eyes Since 1492*. Boston: Houghton-Mifflin, 1992.

DE NIZA, MARCOS (?–1558)

Marcos de Niza was a Franciscan priest who had traveled widely in the Western Hemisphere, including the Caribbean, Guatemala, Peru, and Mexico. In 1538, he was commissioned by the viceroy of Mexico to make a quick exploratory trip to the north of Mexico to find the best route for the Coronado expedition. Rumors of vast wealth in the area—heard by Cabeza de Vaca on his journey across the continent between 1528 and 1536—enticed Francisco Vásquez de Coronado and his troops.

Fray (or Friar) Marcos received permission from Andrés Dorantes to take his Black slave, Estevanico, as his guide. Both Dorantes and Estevanico had accompanied Cabeza de Vaca across the continent. In March 1539, Fray Marcos and Estevanico, along with an escort of Mexican Indians, left Culiacán, Mexico, for the north. On May 21, they reached the Rio Mayo, where they made a fateful decision. Estevanico, who could travel alone much more quickly than the entire party, would scout ahead. It was the last time the party would see Estevanico.

Proceeding north, acquiring an escort of Pimas and Opatas as he traveled, Estevanico reached a Zuni pueblo, possibly Hawikuh, where he demanded women and turquoise from the Zunis. They killed him. When some of Estevanico's party reached Fray Marcos with the news, the priest (according to his account) continued north only far enough to be able to see a pueblo from a hilltop.

Fray Marcos returned to Mexico to give a glowing account of the pueblo he had seen, which he called Cibola. He described it as a city larger than Mexico City, relating that he had heard that it was the smallest of seven large cities in the region. His report quickened Spanish interest in the region and heightened expectations for the gold and the prospects for great wealth that the Coronado expedition might find.

SEE ALSO:
Cabeza De Vaca, Alvar Núñez; Coronado Expedition; Zuni.

DEPARTMENT OF THE INTERIOR

The Department of the Interior was created in 1849 specifically to deal with Indian issues, and so the Bureau of Indian Affairs was transferred into it from the War Department.

Since most of the Indian wars took place after 1849, one might wonder why the responsibility for dealing with Indian issues was taken from the War Department. This change came about for two reasons. By 1849, the United States had completed most of its military campaigns against Mexico and European nations; other Indian nations were no longer needed as military allies, and thus they were no longer thought to be within the purview of the War Department. Also, by 1849, the United States had assumed a proprietary attitude regarding Native people. That is, the United States government now treated Indian people as members of dependent domestic nations, forcing upon them such policies as the removal of entire tribes to Indian Territory (present-day Oklahoma).

Thus, this change in 1849 in U.S. governmental structure to deal with Indian affairs was a reflection

In 1539, Friar Marcos de Niza served as an advance scout for the Coronado expedition. He returned repeating wild rumors he had heard about fabulously rich cities in the present-day North American Southwest.

of changing attitudes and perceptions regarding Indians. They were now viewed as an internal matter of governmental concern, rather than as members of foreign nations. This lack of respect for the sovereignty of Indian nations was a reflection of the attitudes of Manifest Destiny, which had taken a firm grip on American political culture by 1849. (Manifest Destiny was a nineteenth-century belief that the United States had the right and duty to expand throughout the North American continent; for some European-Americans, Manifest Destiny had become a mystical belief that some supernatural force had ordained that the geographical boundaries of the United States should stretch from sea to sea.)

With the conclusion of the war with Mexico in 1848, the only thing standing in the way of a claim

In an effort to force American Indians to assimilate into U.S. culture, the government placed children in boarding schools, away from their families. This photo shows students at an art class at Phoenix Indian School in Arizona in June 1900.

by the United States to being a transcontinental nation was the sovereignty of the many Indian nations on the continent. Thus, the restructuring of the U.S. government in 1849 to deal with Indian issues was a subtle attack on the sovereignty of Indian nations, an attack that would be fully realized in 1873 by act of Congress, which declared that the Congress would no longer make treaties with Indian nations, but would deal with them by unilateral legislative action (a process in which the Indian nations had no voice).

As early as the late 1870s, the commissioners of Indian Affairs believed it was their responsibility to assimilate Indians into American society. "The Indians must conform to 'the white man's ways,' " Commissioner Thomas Jefferson Morgan stated in 1889. Morgan said that Indians must change peaceably "if they will, forcibly if they must."

This attitude was responsible for taking Indian children off their reservations, away from their fam-

ilies, their elders, and their spiritual leaders, and placing them in government-managed boarding schools, all in an effort to assimilate them. Likewise, these attitudes led directly to the forced allotment of Indian lands in the late nineteenth century in Indian Territory, paving the way for the extinguishing of tribal governments and the creation of the state of Oklahoma. On reservations across the rest of the continent, throughout most of the twentieth century, the Department of the Interior continued to pursue a vigorous policy of attempting to assimilate Native peoples into the dominant culture.

In recent years, attitudes have changed within the Interior Department and within the U.S. government. Today, Indians who are regarded highly within their regions are often appointed to the department so that problems caused by past policies and programs might be corrected. Congressional legislation within the last generation has made it possible for Native peoples to practice their Native religions without committing a federal crime. Furthermore, the direct involvement of Indian parents in planning culturally relevant educational programs for Native children in reservation school systems has helped to restore pride in Native cultures and make educational opportunities more accessible for Native children, while still allowing them to remain Indians.

SEE ALSO:
Boarding Schools; Bureau of Indian Affairs; General Allotment Act; Oklahoma; Removal Act, Indian; Termination Policy.

DESKAHEH (1873–1925)

Deskaheh, a Cayuga, also known as Levi General, was *Tadadaho* (speaker) of the Iroquois Grand Council at Grand River, Ontario, in the early 1920s. This was a period when Canadian authorities closed the Longhouse, a traditional form of government, because it had been asserting independence from Canadian jurisdiction. As an alternative, the Canadian authorities proposed to set up a governmental structure that would be responsible to its Indian affairs agency. With Canadian police about to arrest him, Deskaheh traveled to the headquarters of the League of Nations in Geneva, Switzerland, with an appeal for support from the international community.

Several months of effort did not win him a hearing before the international body. This was mostly because of diplomatic manipulation by Britain and Canada, governments that were being embarrassed by Deskaheh and his supporters. When they were unsuccessful in arranging a forum at the League of Nations, Deskaheh and his group organized a private meeting in Switzerland. It drew several thousand people who roared approval of Iroquois sovereignty.

In his last speech, on March 10, 1925, Deskaheh had lost none of this distaste for forced acculturation into the white mainstream. "Over in Ottawa, they call that policy 'Indian Advancement,'" he said. "Over in Washington, they call it 'Assimilation.' We who would be the helpless vic-

tims say it is tyranny. . . . If this must go on to the bitter end, we would rather that you come with your guns and poison gas and get rid of us that way. Do it openly and aboveboard."

As he lay dying, relatives of Deskaheh who lived in the United States were refused entry into Canada to be at his bedside. Deskaheh died two and one-half months after his last defiant speech. His notions of sovereignty have been maintained by many Iroquois into contemporary times. The Iroquois Grand Council at Onondaga issues its own passports, which are recognized by Switzerland and several other countries but not by the United States or Canada.

DE SOTO EXPEDITION

Hernando de Soto (c. 1500–1542) was commissioned by Charles V, Holy Roman emperor and king of Spain, to conquer Florida, with an expedition that would launch from Cuba. (The Spanish called the North American continent *Florida* when viewing it from the perspective of Cuba.) De Soto's expedition would pass through the southeastern portion of the continent at the same time that the expedition of Francisco Vásquez de Coronado was attempting to conquer what is today the southwestern portion of the United States, having launched his expedition from Mexico City.

De Soto was a veteran of Spanish conquest in the Americas, having served in Central America, and having been Francisco Pizarro's cavalry captain in the conquest of the Incas in Peru. These ventures, especially Peru, had made de Soto wealthy. Having been appointed governor of Cuba by Charles V, de Soto now had a chance to invest his personal fortune in the conquest of Florida. Greedily hoping to become even wealthier, de Soto assembled an expedition and in 1538 sailed from Spain for the launching point in Cuba. By 1539, the expedition had landed near Tampa Bay on the Florida coast and fought its way northward to near present-day Tallahassee, where de Soto camped for the winter. From that camp to the next winter camp among the Chickasaws, de Soto left a trail of carnage.

It was a large expedition, which included about 550 soldiers and 200 heavily armored warhorses,

Hernando de Soto became a wealthy man serving under Francisco Pizarro in the conquest of the Incas in Peru. He lost his fortune and his life in a vain search for more wealth in North America.

Muscogee (Creek) country, north into the Cherokee country, back to the south through the land of the Creeks once again, east through the Choctaw country, and north to its second winter camp, among the Chickasaws, in what is today northern Mississippi. On this march, some of the peoples de Soto encountered were prosperous agricultural practitioners of the so-called Temple Mound Culture. By the time later Europeans entered the area, the Temple Mound Culture would be only a distant memory, except for the Natchez culture on the lower Mississippi River.

The de Soto expedition nearly met its end while among the Choctaws. Told to provide women and baggage carriers, Choctaw leader Tuskaloosa told de Soto that he would have them assembled at a town called Moma Bina (near present-day Mobile, Alabama). Instead, however, Tuskaloosa sent word for Choctaw fighting men to assemble at Moma Bina, where they fortified the town and awaited the arrival of de Soto. In the ensuing battle, de Soto's army was able to escape only by setting fire to the town, burning much of its own baggage train in the process. De Soto himself was wounded, and the surviving Spaniards suffered 644 arrow wounds among them, the arrows piercing their skin wherever their armor did not protect them. After burying its dead, the expedition required a month of rest to recover enough to travel. Also killed during the battle were many Choctaws, including their leader, Tuskaloosa.

The Spanish fared no better among the Chickasaws. After a long winter of incessant demands from the Spanish for provisions and servants, the Chickasaws surprised them in the spring by setting fire to their lodgings. Eleven Spaniards were killed, along with nearly all of their horses. Much of the rest of their baggage burned, and for what could be salvaged, such as their swords, a forge had to be constructed to retemper the steel in the blades.

Heading northwest from the Chickasaw country, the expedition built barges and crossed the Mississippi River in June. The Spaniards plundered the villages of the Quapaws in present-day

animals that the indigenous peoples had never seen. The army also included blacksmiths and a forge so that chains could be made as they were needed for the Indian slaves de Soto took to use as servants and baggage carriers. De Soto attempted no diplomacy. Though the people he encountered often greeted him with hospitality and presents, his method was to seize the leader who greeted him, who would then be held hostage, so that de Soto might have a guide to the next town. De Soto's men would then rob the town of all stored foods, pearls, and anything else of value, take slaves for baggage carriers, and then move to the next town.

In this manner, the expedition spent its first year passing through the eastern villages of the

De Soto on the march in North America. He enslaved Indians and made them carry his baggage, until most of the baggage was burned in battles against the Choctaws and Chickasaws.

Arkansas throughout the rest of the year and then wintered there. When de Soto was near the present border between Arkansas and Oklahoma, he was only about 300 miles (480 kilometers) from the Coronado expedition, which at that time was among the Wichita villages of present-day Kansas, along the Arkansas River on the Great Plains. The Coronado expedition had ventured there from the Pueblo country of the upper Rio Grande Valley in present-day New Mexico. There was no contact, however, between the two Spanish expeditions.

Disillusioned at finding nothing that the Spanish valued, and having by then lost half of his men and almost all of his horses, de Soto began his return journey in the spring. When they again reached the Mississippi River, de Soto became sick and died. His men spent the rest of that year attempting to travel west across Louisiana and east Texas, but they returned to the Mississippi and spent most of another year constructing boats. They were finally able to sail down the Mississippi and along the Gulf Coast, until they finally arrived at Vera Cruz, on the coast of Mexico.

The chronicles of the de Soto expedition, particularly one known as the *Gentleman of Elvas*, left valuable records of the Native peoples encountered by de Soto. The expedition also carried with it European diseases that left catastrophic epidemics in its wake. It also brought to the land a new species of animal—hogs—for which the Chickasaws and the Choctaws in particular acquired a fondness. For generations after de Soto passed through their country, Choctaws and Chickasaws would delight in hunting the feral hogs that were one beneficial legacy of the de Soto expedition.

—D. L. Birchfield

SEE ALSO:
Cherokee; Chickasaw; Choctaw; Coronado Expedition; Creek; Five Civilized Tribes; Florida; Inca; Mound Builders; Spain.

SUGGESTED READINGS:
Albornoz, Miguel. *Hernando de Soto: Knight of the Americas*. Translated from the Spanish by Bruce Boeglin. New York: Franklin Watts, 1986.

Bourne, Edward Gaylord, ed. *Narratives of the Career of Hernando de Soto*. New York: Allerton, 1922.

Swanton, John R. *The Indians of the Southeastern United States*. Bureau of American Ethnology, Bulletin Number 137 (1946). Washington, D. C.: Smithsonian Institution Press, 1979.

DIETZ, ANGEL DE CORA
(1871–1919)

Angel De Cora Dietz (Winnebago) was also known as Hinook-Mahiwi-Kilinaka. Born on May 3, 1871, at the Winnebago Agency in Nebraska, she became a noted artist, teacher, and spokesperson for the preservation of Native art. Dietz's mother was a member of the La Mere family; her father was David De Cora, a French-Winnebago descendant of tribal leaders.

In 1883, after attending school on the reservation for a short time, Dietz was taken to the Hampton Normal and Agricultural Institute in Hampton, Virginia, where she completed two terms of study before graduating in 1891. She then continued her education in Massachusetts, first at the preparatory Northampton Classical School for Girls (Miss Burnham's) followed by Smith College, where she earned a degree in art in 1896. She then studied illustration at the Drexel Institute in Philadelphia under the direction of illustrator Howard Pyle. Dietz received further training in Boston at the Cowles Art School and the Museum of Fine Arts School.

Dietz set up an art studio in Boston and later in New York City. She illustrated many publications, including Francis La Flesche's *The Middle Five: Indian Boys of the Omaha Tribe* (1900), Zitkala Sa's *Old Indian Legends* (1901), Natalie Curtis's *The Indians' Book* (1907), and Elaine Goodale Eastman's *Yellow Star: A Story of East and West* (1911). In 1906, she was appointed to head the newly established Department of Native Indian Art at the Carlisle Indian School by U.S. Commissioner of Indian Affairs Francis E. Leupp. She remained in the position until 1915. While at Carlisle, Dietz taught and influenced many students, including William Henry Dietz (Rosebud Sioux), a gifted athlete and artist, who became her husband in 1908.

Dietz worked to preserve Native art through her professional activities, including her charter membership in the Society of American Indians. She also wrote articles on American Indian art, autobiographical sketches, and stories, such as "The Sick Child" and "Grey Wolf's Daughter" (both published in 1899). Dietz, who was divorced in 1918, died of influenza the following year in Northampton, Massachusetts.

SEE ALSO:
Carlisle Indian School; Hampton Institute.

DISEASES

SEE Epidemic Diseases.

DISTRICT OF COLUMBIA

SEE Washington, D.C.

DODGE, HENRY CHEE (1860–1947)

Henry Chee Dodge, who became the first tribal chairman of the Navajo Nation, was born on February 22, 1860. His mother was Bisnayanchi (a Navajo-Jemez Pueblo woman of the Coyote Pass clan), and his father was Juan Anaya, the Mexican silversmith and interpreter for Captain Henry Linn Dodge, the Indian agent to the Navajos. Chee Dodge's father died in 1862, and his mother renamed him after Captain Dodge. As a young lad, he was called Kilchii, or "Red Boy," which is the derivation for his Navajo name "Chee." Dodge also was known as Adits'aii, meaning in Navajo "The Hearing and Understanding Person," and Ashkihih Diitsi, "The Boy Interpreter."

When he was orphaned after the death of his mother during the Navajo Wars of 1863–1866, Chee was taken to Fort Sumner (Bosque Redondo) by his adopted Navajo parents. A few years later, he was adopted by an agency worker, Perry H. Williams, who taught him English. Consequently, he became a useful Navajo interpreter for the U.S. government and a friend of Kit Carson.

On April 19, 1884, Dodge became the successor to the great Navajo chief Manuelito and was made "tribal chief" by Dennis M. Riordan, Superintendent of Indian Affairs. He traveled to Washington, D.C., to meet President Chester A. Arthur shortly after his appointment.

In 1922, Dodge became one of three members of the Navajo "Business Council," which negotiated corporate agreements and investments with economic interests in the area. On July 27, 1923, the Navajo Tribal Council was created, and Chee Dodge was chosen as its first chairman and helped to institute a more formal system of centralized government for the Navajo Nation. Although he stepped down as chairman in 1928, he remained highly influential in tribal affairs.

In 1942, Chee Dodge was elected tribal chairman once again. Even though he was an old man by that time, he journeyed to Washington many times to plead the Navajos' cause. Although he was reelected in 1946, he was never able to take office due to ill health. He was admitted to Sage Memorial Hospital in Ganado, Arizona, with pneumonia and died at the age of eighty-seven on January 7, 1947.

SEE ALSO:
Bosque Redondo; Carson, Kit; Navajo.

DOGS

Dogs were domesticated as early as 6500 B.C.E. The people of the North American continent have had a long and close relationship with dogs. Some American Indians regard the dog as the brother to man.

A Yurok belief holds that if a person talks to a dog, the person will die. In traditional Yurok belief, animal spirits ruled over the earth in prehuman times, and the dogs talked. Eventually, dogs decided to turn the earth over to humans, and the dogs stopped talking. But the belief that it is harmful to talk to dogs still exists.

In the creation account of the Chipewyans, their people were sired by a dog. The Chipewyans, and many other Native peoples, have such a regard for dogs that they are often as well fed and cared for as other members of the tribe. Early French visitors to the Choctaws reported that the Choctaws believed that anyone who had committed murder or who had mistreated their dogs would not find happiness in an afterlife.

Until the modern horse was brought to the continent by Europeans, dogs were the only animals used by North American Plains Indians for hauling loads, moving camp, and hunting. A species of horse was indigenous to the continent, but it had become extinct during the Ice Age.

A large, mature dog could carry 40–50 pounds (18–22 kilograms) of supplies in a pack on its back. More often, however, dogs pulled about 75 pounds (34 kilograms) of supplies loaded onto a sledlike apparatus known as a travois. The travois consisted of two long poles. One end of each pole was attached to the dog's shoulders; the opposite ends trailed on the ground. Netting was placed between the two poles, and supplies were placed on the net. For an extra-heavy load, poles were placed across two travois, and the double travois would be pulled by a pair of dogs.

Plains Indian hunters and their dogs could only travel about six miles (9.5 kilometers) a day because the dogs were not good travelers. Individual dogs and the dogs pulling a travois might fight with one another, and they had to be constantly disciplined and separated. In addition, the dogs might chase after rabbits or wander off to get a drink of water or to investigate something.

Once a buffalo herd was discovered, one method of hunting was for the women to place all of the travois upright into the ground to form a semicircle. Next, the multiple travois would be tied together to make a fence. The women and dogs would then hide behind the fence while two men would run around the buffalo herd, driving the buffalo toward the fence. Other men then closed in as the buffalo neared the fence. The dogs would bark and the women would shout, keeping the buffalo from trampling the fence. All the men would then run toward the buffalo and kill them.

A Navajo boy herds sheep with the help of his dogs on the Navajo Reservation in Arizona.

Inuit with sled dogs in the far north. Teams of this hardy breed of dog can pull a sled for great distances across the frozen landscape.

Dogs were essential in cold regions. The Salish used the fur from a now-extinct breed of dog to make warm blankets. Salt from the urine of a dog was used to bait caribou toward pitfall traps.

Dogs were the only domesticated animals of the Inuit. These Native people had a uniquely interdependent relationship with their specialized dog, called the Eskimo dog or husky.

During a seal hunt, each hunter would have a dog on a leash. With their keen sense of smell, the dogs would go in search of the breathing hole of a seal. As soon as a dog found a breathing hole, it would either lie down or turn around in place. When a seal came to the surface of the hole to breathe, the hunter would be waiting for the kill. The dogs would then drag the day's hunt back to camp.

The Inuit also used Eskimo dogs to pull their sleds. A dog team could haul a sled 20–30 miles (32–48 kilometers) a day. A team of six huskies could pull a lightweight wooden sled. As many as sixteen dogs were needed to pull the sturdier skin-and-bone sled. Each dog team had a lead dog, usually a female. She was the most intelligent of all the dogs. The rest of the dogs both feared and respected her. The lead dog directed the team according to verbal commands or signals from a whip. In eastern areas, dogs were hitched to the sled in a fan-shaped manner. Western Inuit put their dogs in a long, straight line, yoking the dogs together in pairs.

If the Inuit encountered a polar bear during a sled journey, the dogs had an additional duty. They were unleashed and then closed in on the bear, furiously barking and snapping. But the dogs had to be very careful and alert to keep out of the way of the bear's quick and deadly claws. While the dogs distracted the bear in this manner, the hunter went in for the kill with a spear.

Similarly, when the Inuit came upon a herd of musk oxen, the dogs were unleashed. The dogs raced up to the mighty animals and encircled them. While the musk oxen were busy with the dogs, the hunter could kill them from a safe distance with arrows. Today in the far north, dogs are increasingly being replaced by the snowmobile.

— B. Behm

SEE ALSO:
Buffalo; Choctaw; Horses; Inuit.

DONATION LAND ACT OF 1850

In the spring of 1849, a U.S. territorial government was established for the Oregon country, and on September 29 of the following year, Congress passed the Donation Land Act. This act allowed the non-Indian immigrants who were streaming into the country on the Oregon Trail to stake homestead claims to Indian lands even before the land had been ceded by the tribes. In essence, the act offered free land to non-Indians, without anyone having to purchase the land from the tribes or even enter into a treaty with them. It soon caused chaos for tribes throughout the Pacific Northwest.

By the terms of the act, each settler could claim a 320-acre (128-hectare) tract of land. In western Oregon territory, settlers had soon filed 7,437 such claims, amounting to more than 2.25 million acres (900 000 hectares) of land that was still being occupied and used by Native peoples.

In some cases, settlers filed claims that encompassed the principal village site of a tribe. One such claim, filed by A. F. Miller, was for the site of the principal Chetco village. The Chetcos, desiring a peaceful resolution of the issue, surrendered their arms as a show of good faith and their willingness to negotiate. Miller, however, and other whites, desired no negotiations; as soon as the Chetcos were defenseless, they attacked the village, burning the houses and killing fourteen Chetcos.

Scotch Broom on the Oregon coast near Florence. The Donation Land Act of 1850 allowed white settlers to claim these lands from Native peoples, who were driven from their homes without compensation.

Sea stacks near the shore at Bandon Beach on the southern Oregon coast. Native peoples who had harvested the bounty of the sea along the Oregon coast for centuries suddenly had to adjust to a dismal existence on reservations.

In revenge, the Chetcos attacked a detachment of United States Army troops under the command of Lieutenant E. O. Ord, wounding three soldiers and killing one. Six Chetcos were killed in the engagement, and the remaining Chetcos were soon driven from the area, fleeing up the Rogue River. They continued to fight a futile war, which also involved other Native peoples in the area, until 1856, when the Chetcos were the last Indians in southwestern Oregon to surrender. Forced to move to the Grand Ronde Reservation and then to the Coast Reservation (later named the Siletz Reservation), they saw the uncompensated loss of their ancestral lands sanctified by executive order of the president of the United States in 1865 and by act of Congress in 1875. Not until 1946 did the Chetcos receive any compensation for the lost land, when the U.S. Supreme Court upheld a 1945 ruling of the court of claims, which awarded the tribe $489,085.20 for the loss of 433,150 acres (173,260 hectares), a compensation of barely more than one dollar per acre (0.4 hectare).

Other tribes in the Pacific Northwest have experienced delays similar to the Chetcos in receiving compensation for their lost lands. Some compensations have been made by act of Congress. In 1897, Congress authorized a settlement of $10,500 for the Nehalem Tillamook, an Oregon coastal group, and in 1912 another $10,500, also for the Tillamook. These paltry sums did not satisfy either tribe, and in 1962, they successfully prosecuted a joint claim before the Indian Claims Commission for $169,187.50.

Many tribes in the Pacific Northwest have received no compensation for the loss of their lands. The Hanis Coos saw non-Indians stake claims to all of their Coos Bay on the Oregon coast under the Donation Land Act. Desiring no part in the fighting that broke out in southwestern Oregon over the seizures of Indian land under this act, the Hanis managed to survive by allowing themselves to be placed under guard by whites who had formed the Coos County Volunteers. When fighting ended in 1856, the Hanis were marched off to reservations, transferred from one to another, until, in 1875, when the Alsea Reservation was turned over to whites, the Hanis found themselves with no place to live. They returned to the Coos Bay area of their original homeland—but without any tribal lands. In

1916, they prosecuted a claim against the United States for their lost lands, which was not decided by the U.S. Court of Claims until 1938, when the claim was denied because their Indian testimony was ruled inadmissible in court. Despite other evidence, consisting of diaries and records of fur trappers and Indian agents, the U.S. Supreme Court in 1938 refused to hear an appeal of their case, and in 1947 and 1951, the Indian Claims Commission turned them down, saying they had already had their day in court.

Some tribes, such as the Luckiamutes, attempted to gain compensation for their lost lands in treaty negotiations with federal commissioners in 1851, but these negotiations produced nothing when the federal commissioners learned that they were no longer authorized by Congress to negotiate treaties with Indians in the Oregon country. Many of the same tribes, including the Luckiamutes, then negotiated treaties with Anson Dart, Oregon superintendent of Indian affairs, but these treaties were not ratified.

The Luckiamutes were finally able to negotiate a treaty in 1855, which was ratified, with Oregon Superintendent of Indian Affairs Joel Palmer. This treaty provided them with little compensation for their losses but allowed them a place to live on the Grand Ronde Reservation, very near their ancestral homelands. The Grand Ronde Reservation, however, was dissolved in 1955 during the federal government's era of attempting to terminate its relationship with Indian nations.

Throughout the Pacific Northwest, dozens of tribes throughout the Oregon Territory, as it was constituted in 1850, had their land base decimated by the Donation Land Act. They lost even more land through other treaties negotiated in the following years when the Native peoples had already been forced out of their ancestral homes by the claims of settlers under the Donation Land Act.

For many tribes in the region, the passage of the act was a catastrophic event, a severe blow to their ability to conduct their affairs as sovereign nations. Problems of loss and displacement dating from the time the act was passed, and from events that occurred in the aftermath of its passage, continue to plague Native peoples throughout the region. Lack of adequate compensation for their losses and lack of respect on the part of the United States for their rights as sovereign nations have impelled some tribes, such as the Coos, the Kuitsh, and the Siuslaws, to petition, unsuccessfully, for membership in the United Nations.

— D. L. Birchfield

SEE ALSO:
Manifest Destiny; Oregon; Washington State.

SUGGESTED READINGS:

Debo, Angie. *A History of the Indians of the United States.* Norman: University of Oklahoma Press, 1970.

Jaimes, M. Annette, ed. *The State of Native America: Genocide, Colonization and Resistance.* Boston: South End Press, 1992.

Ruby, Robert H., and John A. Brown. *A Guide to the Indian Tribes of the Pacific Northwest.* Rev. ed. Norman: University of Oklahoma Press, 1992.

DORRIS, MICHAEL (1945–)

A well-known author and educator, Michael Anthony Dorris is of mixed Modoc, French, and Irish descent. Born in Dayton, Washington, on January 30, 1945, he is the son of Jim Dorris and Mary Besy (Burkhardt) Dorris.

Dorris earned a bachelor's degree from Georgetown University in 1967, specializing in English and classics, and a master's degree from Yale University in 1970. He also undertook graduate studies in theater and anthropology. Dorris has taught in the anthropology department at Dartmouth College and was instrumental in the development of Dartmouth's Native American studies program.

As a single parent in 1971, he adopted Reynold Abel (referred to in Dorris's writings as Adam) and, later, two other younger Native children, Jeffrey Sava and Madeline Hannah. In 1981, he married the Native poet and fiction writer Louise Erdrich, and they now have three of their own children: Persia Andromeda, Pallas Antigone, and Aza.

Dorris is a prolific and versatile writer, crossing disciplines and formats, including nonfiction, fiction, poetry, and songwriting. He has received numerous literary awards. His academic works include *Native Americans: Five Hundred Years After* (1975) and, with Arlene Hirschfelder and Mary Lou Byler, *A Guide to Research on North American Indians* (1983). His first novel was *A Yellow Raft in Blue Water* (1987). In the autobiographical *The Broken Cord: A Family's Ongoing Struggle with Fetal Alcohol Syndrome* (1989), Dorris relates the impact of fetal alcohol syndrome on his eldest son, Adam. He has coauthored, with Louise Erdrich, *The Crown of Columbus* (1991). His other recent writings include *Morning Girl* (1992), a children's book; *Working Man* (1993), a collection of short fiction; and *Paper Trail* (1994), an anthology of over forty of Dorris's published nonfiction pieces.

SEE ALSO:
Erdrich, Louise; Fetal Alcohol Syndrome; Modoc.

DRAGGING CANOE (c. 1740–1792)

Dragging Canoe is considered by many historians to have been the last great traditional Cherokee war chief. He was born around 1740 in the Cherokee Overhills country, probably in the town of Chota, in the present state of Tennessee. His name, Tsiyugansini, has been translated as "Otter Lifter" and "Arc Bearer," but the most popular and likely the most nearly correct translation is "Dragging Canoe."

The following tale about how he got his name may or may not be true. When he was a small boy, his father and some other men were leaving on a raid. The boy wanted desperately to go along, but his father told him he was too small. The men left, and the boy followed them. His father noticed and ordered him back home. The men went on, and still the boy followed.

At the river's edge, the men picked up their long, heavy dugout canoes and put them in the water. The father noticed that the boy was still with them. At last, he said, "All right. If you can pick up your canoe and put it in the water, you can go along." Thinking that would be the end of it, the father went on about his business. Then one of the other men said, "Look. He is dragging the canoe."

Some historians believe that Dragging Canoe was Shawnee on his mother's side and that when he was a boy in his village, the great Shawnee Tecumseh visited there for a time. It is reasonable to think to think that the boy was profoundly influenced by the presence of the Shawnee leader.

Some historians also believe that Dragging Canoe's father was Attaculaculla (more properly, Ada Gulkula) and that Nancy Ward, known in history as the *ghigau*, usually translated as "Beloved Woman," was either his sister or his cousin. (In the Cherokee clan system, a female first cousin would be called "sister.")

Dragging Canoe first came to prominence in 1775 at Sycamore Shoals, when the old chiefs were tricked into signing away most of Kentucky to representatives of the Transylvania Land Company. Dragging Canoe openly opposed the deal and is reported to have said, "You have bought a fair land, but you will find its settlement dark and bloody."

When settlers moved onto the lands they had illegally purchased from the old men, Dragging Canoe planned his first attack on the American colonists. Nancy Ward learned of the plans, however, and sent warnings to the settlers. Thirteen Cherokee warriors, including Dragging Canoe's brother Little Owl, were killed, and Dragging Canoe was seriously wounded, shot through the hips. He recovered, though, and continued to lead his followers against the colonists.

Strongly opposed to any sale of or encroachment on Cherokee lands, Dragging Canoe and his followers joined forces with England when the colonists rebelled against the British Crown. When their towns were attacked and destroyed by vengeful American rebels, they built new towns along the Chickamauga Creek. Thereafter, Dragging Canoe and his followers were known as Chickamauga Cherokees or simply Chickamaugas. They were not all full-blood Cherokees. Among them were a number of Englishmen, as well as mixed bloods.

When the American Revolution came to an end and other Cherokee towns made peace with the new United States, Dragging Canoe and the Chickamaugas continued to fight. Remembering Tecumseh and his efforts, Dragging Canoe envisioned a large alliance of Indian tribes to oppose further U.S. expansion into Indian lands, but he was kept too busy fighting to devote much time to the plan.

When Dragging Canoe died in 1792, at around fifty-two years of age, he had been fighting colonial and U.S. expansion for fifteen years. The lead-ership of the Chickamaugas passed into the hands of John Watts and Bob Benge, both mixed-blood Cherokees. Benge was killed in 1794, and without the strong leadership of Dragging Canoe, even the Chickamaugas at last gave up the fight against the United States. They signed a treaty in 1794, and in that same year many of them moved west with Chief Bowles to form the Western Cherokee Nation, first in Missouri and then in Arkansas. The Cherokee Nation never again took up arms against the United States.

— R. J. Conley

SEE ALSO:
Cherokee; Tecumseh; Ward, Nancy.

DRED SCOTT DECISION

The Dred Scott decision, officially known as *Dred Scott v. Sandford*, was an important United States Supreme Court ruling on the issue of slavery. The decision reveals racial attitudes toward nonwhites in the United States at about the time that removal to Indian Territory was forced upon the Indian nations of the Southeast.

Dred Scott was a slave owned by John Emerson, a U.S. Army surgeon in Missouri. In 1834, Emerson moved Scott with him when he transferred to a post in Illinois, a free state, and again when he moved into Wisconsin Territory, free under the Missouri Compromise. The Missouri Compromise of 1820 prohibited slavery in U.S. territory north of 36°30' north latitude. They returned to Missouri, a slave state, in 1838. After Emerson died, Scott sued Emerson's widow for his freedom. Scott argued that he was free by reason of his residence in free territory.

Scott won his case in the lower state court, but the Missouri Supreme Court overturned the ruling in 1852 and said that Scott was still a slave. By this time, Emerson's widow had remarried, and his estate was administered by his brother, John Sanford (misspelled Sandford in Supreme Court records). Because Sanford did not live in Missouri, Scott's attorneys successfully moved the case into federal district court. The federal court ruled against Scott, and the case went on to the U.S. Supreme Court.

The Supreme Court ruling was handed down on March 6, 1857; the Court split seven to two against Scott. In his opinion, Chief Justice Roger Taney came to the following conclusions: First, persons of African descent, whether free or not, had no rights of U.S. citizenship and therefore Scott was not entitled to bring suit in federal court. Second, Scott was not made free by living in free territory because the antislavery legislation of the Missouri Compromise was unconstitutional. Congress could not deprive a slave owner of his right to own property. And finally, Scott had ultimately returned to Missouri and was therefore subject to the laws of that state.

At this time, the country was in great debate over the slavery issue. The Missouri Compromise had supposedly settled the issue, but the addition of new territories to the nation had renewed the controversy. It was hoped the Dred Scott decision would put the matter to rest, but instead it heated up the tensions between the proslave South and abolitionists in the North. This helped push the country closer to civil war and influenced the later passage of the Fourteenth Amendment, which, in part, made former slaves U.S. citizens.

The Dred Scott case had little direct bearing on the lives of American Indians of the day, despite whatever interest they might have had in the plight of an African-American at the hands of European-Americans and their laws. The case is of interest to students of Native American history, however. In addition to providing a look at the racial climate in the United States at the time, the case took place when the United States was adding new territories, and with them a jumble of competing laws and jurisdictions in which cases like this were being played out and debated. And these territories—like the lives that were being disrupted and in many cases destroyed—had once been Indian America.

This handheld drum from the Great Lakes region was crafted by Anishinabe people (also known as Chippewa or Ojibwe).

DRESS

SEE Regalia.

DRUMS

A drum can be something as simple as a log, or it can be as elaborate as a beautifully made ceremonial drum with painted rawhide heads. Drums are constructed in all fashions and designs—from small drums, such as the peyote drum, the Mandan Turtle Drum, the Cherokee Water Drum, or the Acoma and Yuchi Clay Pot Drum, to the giant "big drums" of the powwow and other large social gatherings throughout North America.

For many years, the Iroquois have been making water drums out of tiny kegs, or firkins, and fastening the heads in place with iron hoops made by their blacksmiths. Cherokees made very small water drums, tiny enough to be held in a person's hand.

Drums are a vital part of many contemporary Native ceremonials. Some ceremonials can be performed publicly, such as this display of Inuit drum singing at the Inuit Indian Olympics in Fairbanks, Alaska.

The Cherokees preferred the skin of a woodchuck for the drumhead because it is thin but very tough.

Water drums were popular because the drummer could vary the tone of the drum by pouring water on the head while beating the drum. In a damp climate, this was something to consider because the rawhide heads on larger drums often go "flat" when damp. In addition to providing a variety of tones, a rawhide drum was a good weather forecaster because it often might go "flat" when it became damp, thus helping to predict coming storms. Water drums were played near heat or fire so that as the head dried out, the tone rose to a higher pitch. Then, it was tipped to splash the water on the head again, and the tone instantly dropped back to its original level.

The larger drums, mostly called "big drums," are usually referred to as rawhide drums. They are normally seen at powwows and social gatherings. These drums require a larger type of animal skin to wrap around the hull of the drum. These skins usually came from deer or buffalo hides. The larger drums have a softer head and must be dry when drumming. The drumsticks—the sticks that the drummers use to beat the drum—are usually constructed of soft material (mostly animal hair) that add padding at the end of the stick. Sometimes the way in which a drumstick is made can be just as important as how the drum is made. The big drum can accommodate from eight to fifteen singers sitting together in circular formation around the drum, all drumming and singing in harmony. Others at the gathering respond to the rhythm of the beat, to this "voice of thunder," as they would to an invitation—some would call it a command—to start dancing.

Foot drums are drums that are large enough for individuals to dance on. In California, the Maidus used half of a hollow sycamore log, 5 or 6 feet (1.5 to 1.8 meters) long, placed over a trench. This drum was actually played by someone who danced on it in time to the song. Sometimes, at the same time, two or three men also beat upon the drum with heavy sticks or clubs.

These drummers are participating in the Deer Dance at Santa Clara Pueblo in New Mexico.

A Plains Indian drum. Many drums were seized from Native people and placed in museums. Today, Native people are attempting to have many of their ceremonial objects returned to them.

The most common drum, the hand drum, is constructed with skin stretched across one or both sides of the small drum. Hand drums with skin on just one side are referred to as "open-faced." The quality of the sound of an open-faced hand drum, including the tone and pitch of the drumbeat, is quite different from that of a two-faced hand drum.

In the Southwest, ceremonial drums are usually made of hollow logs like cottonwood and occasionally oak, with two heads completely laced over on both ends. Pueblo drums have a log frame or shell that is about twice as long as the diameter of the heads. Pueblo drums are also regarded as sacred, and individuals take great care of their drums.

Some designs are painted on the drums, usually on its face. The designs or symbols are those of the drum makers or owner of the drum. Whether the song is interpreted literally as referring to events of the past or figuratively for the present, many singers and dancers know the meaning of the drum songs. When they hear the beat of the big drum, their imagination is focused upon a significant emotion that is associated with that song.

All drums were regarded as having sacred or mysterious power, and not just anybody was able to own, play, or even care for a ceremonial drum. Special protection and care were usually designated to a responsible individual, a special officer called the "Drum Keeper," who both understood the sacred quality of the big drum and regarded the drum as a personality in need of special care. In some tribes, the drum was treated like a person, kept in a secure place in the lodge in a place of honor, and offered food and drink to support its spirit. The responsibility to care for the drum was perpetually held by a family within an extended family structure.

Old ceremonial drums were usually made of rolled-up rawhide covering a circular object. Sometimes wooden slats were used to tie down the drum, while the singers beat in unison with the songs. With larger drums, like those used in powwows, singers usually sit side by side and rather close while facing the drum. Before the singing begins, some singers offer tobacco to the drum. This gesture honors the drum and allows the singers to sing clearly and the dancers to have good feelings throughout the ceremony. Some tribal groups use other plants like sweet grass, sage, or corn to honor the drum.

Drums carry the rhythm of a ceremony by drumbeats. Dancers are moved by the meaning of the rhythm in the drum's pattern and sound. Most Indian rhythm patterns are chanted, drummed, or made by shaking rattles. The patterns of the drum are usually simple and composed of steady beats. Sometimes the more complicated rhythm of drumbeats involves a drumroll, rests, and short and long beats.

It takes many years of concentration and practice to coordinate singing and drumming at the same time. Along with drumming, tribal traditions include chants evolving into songs containing various patterns of mythological cycles, recitations of events that take place in a visionary or superhistorical world. Other meanings come from invocations of the helping spirits, sometimes referred to as the "Great Spirit." Most drumming is an expression of gratitude for what has been given to us as human beings. Whatever the situation, the drum forges a connection between the spirit and human worlds.

Although there is a certain artificiality in making divisions between northern and southern tribal groups and traditions—particularly when some of the midwestern and southeastern tribes include elements common to both northern and southern groups—the normal assumption remains that such divisions do often hold true. Northern traditions normally represent the sub-Arctic regions down through southern Canada and parts of the upper United States, while the southern traditions are in the southern part of the United States.

In the arena of intertribal singing and dancing, two major forms of styles are presented by regional significance of dress and dance movement. The two traditions that have formed as a result of collective similarities of dancing have become known as "Northern" and "Southern" Plains' Indian traditions. Most of the Northern drums, of course, come from the northern states like North Dakota, South Dakota, Minnesota, and Montana. Southern drums are usually those drums that represent the southern states, mostly from Oklahoma.

It is very important to honor the drum by respecting its significance to song and dance. Therefore, no Indian drum should be called or referred to as a *tom-tom*. This term came from the English-speaking people and has no meaning or relevance to traditional Indian people.

— C. Pewewardy

SEE ALSO:
Dance, American Indian; Regalia.

DULL KNIFE (c. 1810–1883)

Dull Knife and Little Wolf were the two principal Cheyenne leaders who led the trek back to their homeland in eastern Montana after the Cheyennes' exile to Indian Territory (later called Oklahoma) late in the 1870s and 1880s. The Lakotas called him "Dull Knife," while the Cheyennes called him "Morning Star."

The beginning of the end of freedom for Dull Knife and his band in their Montana homeland began when Colonel Ranald S. Mackenzie moved out of Fort Fetterman in November 1876. As Mackenzie searched for Crazy Horse's Oglalas, he ran into Dull Knife's band. Nearly half of Mackenzie's force was made up of reservation-bound Cheyennes and Pawnees recruited from near-starving conditions. Mackenzie's force devastated Dull Knife's band of four hundred warriors. A group of survivors hobbled to Crazy Horse's camp at Beaver Creek. Eleven children froze to death during the march, and the Cheyennes ate nearly all their horses.

In the spring of 1877, the Cheyennes who had lodged with Crazy Horse during the winter surrendered to General Nelson Miles at Fort Keough. The rest were sent to Darlington Reservation, Indian Territory. With growing bitterness, Dull Knife realized that promises of abundant game in Oklahoma were a lie. The buffalo were gone, and smaller game had been hunted to near extinction by Indians sent there earlier. Cheyennes also began to die of a fever, probably malaria; others starved. Promised government rations did not arrive on time.

In the middle of August 1878, Dull Knife and Little Wolf pleaded with Indian agent John Miles to let the Cheyennes return home. Half the band had died in a year in Oklahoma, and Dull Knife himself was shaking with fever as they talked. Miles asked for a year to work on the problem, and Little Wolf told him the Cheyennes would be dead in a year. Miles refused to relent.

The next morning at sunrise, the 300 surviving Cheyennes broke for the open country, heading for their home on the Powder River, a thousand miles away. At White Clay Creek, Nebraska, the Cheyennes split into two groups: Dull Knife and 150 others went into Red Cloud Agency to surrender; Little Wolf and a roughly equal number headed into the Nebraska Sand Hills, where they spent the winter in hiding.

Back in Nebraska, Dull Knife's band had found Red Cloud Agency abandoned so they moved on to Fort Robinson. For two months, Dull Knife's

Cheyennes lived at the fort while the commanding officer awaited orders. When they finally came, the orders were to send the Indians back to Indian Territory. Dull Knife refused to go: "No! I am here on my own ground, and I will never go back. You may kill me here, but you cannot make me go back!" Captain Wessells, the commanding officer, sought to make the Cheyennes change their minds by locking them in a freezing barracks with no food or water. For three days, the Cheyennes remained in the barracks in below-freezing weather. Wessells gave them a last chance to surrender, and the Cheyennes again refused.

Just after sunset on January 9, 1879, Little Shield, a Dog Soldier Society leader, helped the Cheyennes in a desperate breakout. The Dog Soldiers led people out of the barracks' windows. Soldiers chased them out of the fort, shooting wildly. Fifty Cheyennes died in the snow that evening, and twenty more died of wounds and exposure. Most of the remaining Cheyennes, fewer than a hundred now, were herded back to Fort Robinson.

Dull Knife, his wife, and son were among the few who escaped. They walked eighteen nights, resting by day, to Pine Ridge. They ate bark and their own moccasins to survive. At the Pine Ridge Agency, Bill Rowland, an interpreter, took the family in. The harrowing march back to the Cheyenne homeland is described in Mari Sandoz's novel *Cheyenne Autumn*.

SEE ALSO:
Cheyenne; Crazy Horse.

DUST BOWL

The term *dust bowl* usually refers to a region that has been reduced to an extremely dry state by drought and dust storms. In the United States, *Dust Bowl* refers to a period in which a terrible drought hit the Southern Plains area in the early 1930s. It was a nightmare for landowners and farmers as strong

Giant dust storms such as the one pictured above made the southern Great Plains nearly uninhabitable during much of the 1930s. Many Native people from the region moved to California during that time.

winds swept over the dry land and buried fields, fences, and houses under drifts of dust. Millions of acres (hectares) were abandoned by poverty-stricken families.

The nightmare of the Dust Bowl covered the Plains in western Kansas, southeastern Colorado, western Oklahoma, northeastern New Mexico, and Texas. Cattle and poultry died, and people became poor, hungry, and desperate. A child returning from school was found buried under dust less than half a mile (0.8 kilometer) from his home.

For the American Indians living in this region, times were exceptionally difficult. Even though the Plains had experienced drought when the buffalo and cattle grazed the tall grasses, farmers plowing the land destroyed the protective prairie grasses. During this time of despair, California lured Indians and non-Indians alike. But Native people left their former reservation homes for the West only to find jobs as migrant farmworkers or in some other area of manual labor.

Long days and little pay resulted in extreme poverty conditions. Still, the mass media reported conditions in California as superior with good pay, plenty of food, and nice living conditions. Those in the Dust Bowl who felt the pain of poverty left in droves to find their place in the sun. American Indians found themselves and their children living in shacks with no running water, electricity, or cooking stoves. Their work was hard, the days were long, and the pay was less than minimal. Some families resorted to eating sparrows, and so terrible were the living and working conditions, that some of those who grew up in the orchards cannot stand the smell of apples or peaches to this day.

Most families could not obtain the money to get back to their homes in the Plains and had to remain in their poverty-stricken conditions. Eventually, people began grouping together and relating their common beliefs and interests to one another, in time creating some of the most effective and positive urban agencies in the nation. Their interrelating as they traveled from orchard to farm gave Native people a closeness and recognition of one another that spread throughout the state of California.

Through agricultural programs and other government methods, but mostly by nature, the Dust Bowl subsided. The battle became less difficult by the late 1930s.

SEE ALSO:
Social Conditions.

DUTCH COLONISTS

The Dutch arrived on the shores of North America with the first wave of colonists. From 1614 to 1664, and again briefly from 1673 to 1674, the Dutch held the colony they called New Netherland, which included the Hudson Valley and the area of present-day New York City. Chartered by the West India Company, the Dutch established a trading post colony. They aspired to control the commerce of North America, in particular the fur trade. They were entranced with the idea of a new country with no stores and no merchants.

The Dutch focus on trade affected relations with the Native peoples. Good mutual connections are important between merchant and customer and between supplier and merchant. The Iroquois provided fur pelts to the Dutch. In turn, the Dutch armed the Iroquois with rifles. In addition, because the number of Dutch colonists never grew as large as that of some of the other European groups, their generally cordial relations with the Indians were based on a heightened sense of self-preservation. Indeed, the Dutch forged an alliance with the Iroquois that was never broken because the Iroquois were too powerful.

While the Dutch traders did not make a practice of visiting Indian villages or marrying into Native American families, they did encourage Native Americans to visit their trading posts. During the trading season of May through November, hundreds of Native people arrived in Fort Orange (present-day Albany), where temporary dwellings were constructed for them. Although historians have commented that the Dutch established better relations with their Native neighbors than the English, the results were ultimately the same. That is, over time the Native peoples were decimated by disease from contact with the Dutch, and they eventually lost their lands through warfare and treaty.

Dutch settlement increased slowly because initially the Dutch had little interest in acquiring land. In fact, they usually established settlements only as a way of claiming land in the face of increasing

This drawing depicts Dutch merchants trading with Indians on Manhattan Island. These early contacts transmitted European diseases that decimated Native populations.

English and French resistance to their business activities. This began to change in 1639 when the West India Company abandoned the fur trade monopoly and offered new incentives for colonists, including two hundred acres (eighty hectares) of land for each head of household. With expanded settlement, friction grew between the Dutch and the Native peoples. In the Dutch view, once the Hudson Valley had been trapped out, its only value was as farmland. This meant that the local tribes were no longer necessary for trapping and trading furs and so were seen as an obstacle.

Willem Kieft, director general of New Netherland, foolishly launched the Dutch into war with their Native neighbors by levying a tax on them. After a few incidents of vandalism in reaction to this policy, the Dutch led a punitive expedition against the Indians of Staten Island. In 1640, Kieft offered a bounty for every Raritan's head delivered to the fort at New Amsterdam. After a retaliatory murder of an old Dutch wheelwright, Kieft ordered a military action that became known as the Battle

of Pavonia. In this battle, soldiers massacred the inhabitants of a Lenape village and burned their structures. After the massacre, a full-scale war erupted in 1643, and a combined Dutch-English force destroyed Native villages at Fort Neck, Hempstead, and Pound Ridge. The West India Company, displeased with Kieft's actions and the costliness of the wars, replaced him in 1647 with Peter Stuyvesant.

Stuyvesant dealt with the Native peoples more through negotiation and less through confrontation. Also, Stuyvesant's attention was turned to the English encroachment on the Dutch colony. In 1650, the Treaty of New Hartford established boundaries between New Netherland and New England, resulting in a loss of land for the Dutch. The First Anglo-Dutch War broke out in 1652.

Despite these conflicts, Dutch immigration continued to increase, and business prospered. The Dutch sent home forty-three thousand fur pelts every year from the Fort Orange trading post alone. The retreat of the frontier settlers to towns during the last Dutch-Indian conflict, coupled with the devastation of many local tribes due to disease, played a part in maintaining peace between the two groups for a while.

Increased settlement, however, led to more friction between the Dutch and their Native neighbors. In 1655, when Peter Stuyvesant and his troops were completing an expedition to annex New Sweden to New Netherland, a combined force of Mahican, Pachami, Esopus, and Hackensack Indians attacked Manhattan Island. Avoiding the cities, they destroyed farms and orchards in what came to be known as the Peach Tree War. In succeeding years, the First and Second Esopus Wars were fought at Wiltwyck (now Kingston, New York), begun by the Esopus after being harassed by the Dutch settlers. The peace treaty signed in 1664 ended the Native American dominance of the region. The Mahican and various Lenape groups were forced to cede most of their ancestral lands to the Dutch.

Three months after the conclusion of the long, bloody, exhausting wars with the Native peoples, the Dutch themselves were conquered by the English. With the exception of the recapture of New Netherland in 1673, which lasted only fifteen months, the political influence of the Dutch in North America was at an end.

— M. A. Stout

SEE ALSO:
Colonialism; Iroquois Confederacy; New York.

DUWAMISH

The ancestral homeland of the Duwamish is on Puget Sound in the present state of Washington. The Duwamish are now a landless tribe, unrecognized by the United States. They received no compensation for the loss of their land until 1962, when the U.S. Indian Claims Commission awarded them $1.35 an acre for 54,790 acres (21,916 hectares). This land now constitutes the city of Seattle, which was named for Duwamish chief Sealth (Seattle).

The principal Duwamish village site was at the outlet of Lake Washington. Pioneer Square, where settlers laid the foundations for the city of Seattle, was a Duwamish winter village site. Many of their other village sites have been inundated by massive changes wrought by the U.S. Army Corps of Engineers in 1916, which altered the Duwamish and Cedar Rivers and caused the Black River to no longer exist.

Chief Seattle tried to maintain friendly relations with the non-Indians who were streaming

Lake Washington, in the city of Seattle, with the Olympic Mountains in the background. Lake Washington was the home of the Duwamish until they were forced to flee from their homeland.

into the Oregon country. Shortly after the territory of Washington was organized in 1853 from the northern portion of Oregon Territory, he entered into a treaty of peace and friendship with the United States in 1855 at Port Elliott.

When hostilities broke out in 1856 involving a number of area tribes, including some Duwamish, Chief Seattle attempted to intercede. Despite his help, the Duwamish were removed to a reservation across Puget Sound on the Kitsip Peninsula, where they experienced friction with the resident Suquamish.

All but a few families of Duwamish fled the reservation at the outbreak of hostilities in 1856, first to Bainbridge Island for a few months, then to Elliot Bay. From there, the government removed them to Holdeness Point, but they soon returned to their ancestral homeland on the Duwamish River. Some Duwamish were resettled on the Muckleshoot Reservation, but most Duwamish remained in what had become the western portion of the city of Seattle until whites burned them out of their homes in 1893, and they fled to Ballast Island.

In 1925, the Duwamish adopted a constitution and formed a government but were denied federal recognition. A Duwamish claim filed with the court of claims in 1926 for compensation for loss of land was denied after being in the judicial system for ten years. A subsequent claim filed in 1946 with the Indian Claims Commission finally resulted in the 1962 award of only $1.35 an acre for 54,790 acres (21,916 hectares) for the loss of the land in Seattle that the commission ruled the tribe had owned in 1856.

The tribe appealed the decision to the court of claims, but the court upheld the decision of the Indian Claims Commission. In 1973, citing their lack of federal recognition and their landlessness, the courts denied them the right to participate with other tribes in the catch of up to half of the annual harvest of salmon and steelhead trout in Washington State.

The Duwamish have established a nonprofit corporation that seeks to maintain the tribal culture and engage in projects to support the tribe's independence. Some Duwamish are enrolled on the Muckleshoot and Suquamish reservations and are thereby able to gain access to Indian Health Services, but they cannot identify themselves as Duwamish.

SEE ALSO:
Federally Recognized Nations and Tribes; Washington Coast and Puget Sound Indians, History of; Washington State.

EAGLE FEATHERS

SEE Feathers and Featherwork.

EARTH LODGE

As they traveled along the Missouri and Republican Rivers, early European explorers found villages of agricultural peoples who lived in homes dug into the earth of the Plains. These "earth lodges" served as a model for early European-American colonizers in areas such as Nebraska. The settlers reacted to a shortage of wood and the lack of facilities to make bricks by constructing what they called "sod houses."

As with other types of housing on the Plains, such as tipis and grass houses, the earth lodges built by Native peoples were constructed and maintained with attention to their spiritual beliefs. Earth lodges were often arranged in patterns that illustrated a particular people's class structure or relationship to the universe. Among the Mandan, for example, earth lodges along the upper Missouri River were built around a plaza, with the highest-ranking religious officials closest to the center. Lodges, like tipis, were sometimes constructed in a circle to signify a people's vision of a unified cosmos.

Earth lodges first appeared about 700 B.C.E. in the earliest agricultural settlements of the Great Plains. The Dakotas, Mandans, Hidatsas, Omahas, Poncas, Otos, Arikaras, and others erected villages of earth lodges along the streams that emptied into the Missouri River. Most of the peoples who constructed earth lodges had more than one home. That is, they farmed in the summer and sometimes lived by hunting in the winter, when cultivated food was scarce. In the summer, the people who lived in the lodges grew several types of corn and beans, as well as squash and tobacco. Many of their villages were surrounded by log walls for protection from outside attack. In winter, many villages moved

Interior of a Mandan earth lodge on the Missouri River. These structures provided shelter from the brutal winters on the northern Great Plains.

to smaller earth lodges nearer the river because firewood was abundant there and the valleys were sheltered from the strongest of the Plains' winter winds.

Most of the lodges were constructed by first driving four or more logs (usually cottonwood) into the ground, then joining them with cross beams. Wood was added to form a roughly rectangular frame and then covered with earth and grass. The earliest earth lodges were rectangular; over time, the design became more circular. Sometimes, a layer of wet earth was allowed to dry on top of the earth lodge to help seal out moisture. The earth lodges were remarkably well insulated against the extreme heat and cold of the Plains climate, and their design has been studied recently for clues to energy-efficient home construction.

SEE ALSO:
Architecture, Indian; Arikara; Hidatsa; Mandan; Omaha; Ponca; Siouan Nations.

EARTHQUAKES

Earthquakes have affected the lives of Native peoples in the Americas for thousands of years, and on occasion, they have played a role in altering the course of history. Phenomena such as earthquakes, volcanic eruptions, hurricanes, and tornadoes also had to be accounted for in the cosmology of Native peoples (that is, the view of the universe held by Native peoples), and the artistic and creative responses to these phenomena are as richly varied as the many different indigenous cultures in the hemisphere.

Earthquakes are a part of the natural environment throughout the hemisphere, but they occur with greatest frequency along the Pacific coasts of North and South America and of Asia and Eurasia, where the "ring of fire" encircles the Pacific Ocean basin. The slippage of continental plates at the edges of the Pacific Ocean create frequent

For thousands of years, Native peoples in California have had to contend with earthquakes, such as this one that hit Northridge, California, in 1993.

Catholic priests who were working among them. The frightening intensity of this quake was seized upon by the priests in an effort to spread fear among the Chelans and aid the efforts of the priests in getting new converts to Catholicism. Nmosize, a Chelan leader and a defender of Native beliefs, responded to the tactic of the priests by burning down their mission house. Afterward, the priests abandoned such crude tactics, and relations with the Chelans were repaired, with the priests proceeding in a more dignified manner.

The same quake caused a much more severe disruption in the lives of the Entiats. The ancestral home of the Entiats had been along the lower reaches of the Entiat River, near its confluence with the Columbia River, until many of them were relocated to the area of Lake Chelan by the terms of the Yakima Treaty of 1855. Some Entiats also moved upstream on the Columbia, including Nicterwhilicum, also known as Wapato John, who settled on the banks of the river. On November 14, 1872, the quake dislodged the Ribbon Cliffs, temporarily damming the Columbia and flooding the Entiats out, ruining all of their improvements and forcing them to move again.

destructive earthquakes. Quakes in China have killed hundreds of thousands of people at one time. A quake in Alaska in 1962, the strongest ever recorded in modern times in North America, devastated the city of Anchorage. Many dangerous fault zones underlie California. All along the Pacific rim, whether in Mexico, Peru, or Chile, quakes are frequent and can be of disastrous intensity.

The large earthquake of November 14, 1872, in Washington State might serve as an example of how quakes have affected Native peoples in recent times. The epicenter of the quake was in north-central Washington, east of the Cascades, in the land of the Chelans, who speak a Wenatchee dialect of the Interior Salishan language. The quake played a role in straining relations between the Chelans and Roman

Though the Pacific Coast has a high frequency of earthquakes, the interior of North America contains some faults that may be more potentially devastating. An earthquake on December 5, 1811, centered in the southeastern portion of the present state of Missouri, is believed to have been the most violent earthquake in the recent history of the continent. No seismic instruments recorded the quake, but another kind of apparatus, church bells, did record its tremor. The quake rang church bells as far away as Boston, Massachusetts. Near its epicenter, it caused the Mississippi River to flow backward, and it dislodged cliffs and split the earth with such violence that the course of the Mississippi was altered in many places. If the present cities of Memphis and St. Louis had existed at that time, the devastation would have been severe.

The quake also had an impact on the history of Native peoples in the Southeast, particularly the Creeks. Shawnee leader Tecumseh, concluding his visit to the Creeks in November 1811, attempted to recruit them into his pan-Indian alliance by telling them that they would know when he had returned safely to his home because he would stamp his foot on the ground. The quake, occurring at just about the time it would take Tecumseh to return home, startled the Creeks, roused them out of their lodges, and made true believers out of many of them, who were known as the Red Sticks. The Red Stick faction of the Creeks likely would have supported Tecumseh's vision for a pan-Indian alliance anyway, but the earthquake, coming as it did, made them fanatical believers, and they pursued that vision vigorously until it was shattered at the Battle of Horseshoe Bend.

Today, more than half of all Native people live in urban areas, and many from all areas of the continent have migrated to the large urban centers in California. This is where the frequency of earthquakes and the potential for a truly devastating one on the San Andreas fault make Native people among the highest percentage of ethnic groups at risk from the violence of earthquakes on the North American continent.

— D. L. Birchfield

SEE ALSO:
Pan-Indian (Intertribal) Movements; Tecumseh.

EASTMAN, CHARLES
(1858–1939)

Charles Eastman, a Santee Sioux, provided, along with his contemporaries Luther Standing Bear and Gertrude Bonnin, an historical voice for the Sioux during the generations after

subjugation by the United States. Eastman also was educated as a medical doctor and was a founder of the Society of American Indians.

Eastman was born near Redwood Falls, Minnesota; he was four years old when his family was involved in the 1862 Great Sioux Uprising in Minnesota. The family fled to Canada with other Santee Sioux, but Eastman's father was later turned over to United States authorities. His father was among the Sioux who were sentenced to hang, but he was pardoned along with others by President

Dr. Charles Eastman in 1922, in dress rehearsal for a play to be performed during the St. Nicholas Festival in New York.

Abraham Lincoln. His death sentence was commuted to a prison term.

Eastman was raised by relatives near Fort Ellis, in southern Manitoba. Known in adulthood by the Sioux name Ohiyesa ("The Winner"), Eastman attended Dartmouth College, entering the freshman class of 1883 and graduating in 1887. Eastman earned a medical degree from Boston University in 1890, at the same time that he provided eyewitness reporting of the Wounded Knee massacre. Later, he was a government physician at Pine Ridge in South Dakota during a time when epidemics were still sweeping reservation-bound Indians. Eastman later turned to private practice and still later, with encouragement from his wife Elaine Goodale, to writing and lecturing.

Eastman was an unusually brilliant student as a young man. He was the person most responsible for the incorporation of Indian lore into the Boy Scouts of America. Eastman wrote nine books, some of which were translated into several languages other than English. Two of his books were autobiographical: *Indian Boyhood* (1902) and *From the Deep Woods to Civilization* (1916).

SEE ALSO:
Bonnin, Gertrude; Sioux Uprising (1862); Standing Bear, Luther.

ECOLOGY, NATIVE AMERICAN CONCEPTIONS OF

Although Native Americans lived in roughly two thousand distinct societies and spoke several hundred mutually unintelligible languages at the time of first sustained contact with Europeans, these diverse cultures all shared ways of life that involved symbiosis with the natural world.

Luther Standing Bear, who watched the early years of settlement on the Plains, contrasted the Euro-American and Native American conceptions of the natural world of North America: "We did not think of the great open plains, the beautiful rolling hills, and winding streams with tangled brush, as 'wild.' Only to the white man was nature 'a wilderness' and only to him was the land 'infested' with 'wild' animals and 'savage' people.

In 1928, the Sioux at Rosebud, South Dakota, were allowed to perform the Sun Dance for the first time in twelve years, for the benefit of Senator Charles Curtis *(right)*, a candidate for vice president of the United States. For much of the nineteenth and twentieth centuries, Sioux culture, including many of its sacred ceremonies, was vigorously repressed by the U.S. government.

These dancers are participating in the Corn Dance at Zuni Pueblo in New Mexico. Festivals celebrating and affirming people's relationship with agriculture have been an integral part of Pueblo culture for many generations.

To us it was tame. Earth was bountiful, and we are surrounded with the blessings of the Great Mystery."

Vine Deloria, Jr., documents the natural metaphor of earth as mother as far back as 1776. On June 21, at a conference in Pittsburgh during the American Revolution, Cornstalk, who was trying to convince the Mingos [Iroquois] to ally with the Americans, said, "You have heard the good Talks which our Brother [George Morgan] Weepemachukthe ["The White Deer"] has delivered to us from the Great Council at Philadelphia representing all our white brethren who have grown out of this same ground with ourselves, for this Big [Turtle] Island being our common Mother, we and they are like one Flesh and Blood."

Most Native peoples worked nature into their rituals and customs because their lives depended on the bounty of the land around them. Where a single animal comprised the basis of a Native economy (such as the salmon of the Pacific Northwest or the buffalo on the Plains), strict cultural sanctions came into play against killing of animals in numbers that would exceed their natural replacement rate.

On the Plains, the military societies of the Cheyennes, Lakotas, and other peoples enforced rules against hunting buffalo out of season and against taking more animals than were necessary for survival.

The Sun Dance ceremonies of the Plains reflect a celebration of the cycle of life. Like the Christian Easter, the Sun Dance, which the

Cheyennes call the "New Life Lodge," is associated with the return of green vegetation and the increase in animal populations (especially the buffalo) during the spring and early summer. The ritual is communal, and it expresses a tribe or nation's unity with the earth and dependence on it for sustenance.

In some parts of the Sun Dance, the skin is pierced, but those parts are not required of anyone not wishing to participate in them. In some ways, the central purpose of the Sun Dance is similar to that of the First Salmon Ceremony: Each is part of a cycle of life and sustenance and reflects the respect for a people's main food source. The Sun Dance pole is said to unite sky and earth; the four sacred directions also are part of the ceremonial design.

Corn, the major food source for several agricultural peoples across the continent, also enjoyed a special spiritual significance. Corn and beans (which grow well together because the beans, a legume, fix nitrogen in their roots) were often said to maintain a spiritual union.

Some peoples, such as the Omahas of the eastern Great Plains, "sang up" their corn through special rituals. In addition to "singing up the corn," the Pueblos cleaned their storage bins before the harvest, "so the corn will be happy when we bring it in." The Pawnees grew ten varieties of corn, including one (called "holy" or "wonderful" corn) that was used only for religious purposes and never eaten.

The Mandans had a Corn Priest who officiated at rites during the growing season. Each stage of the corn's growth was associated with particular songs and rituals, and spiritual attention was said to be as important to the corn as proper water, sun, and fertilizer. Among the Zunis, a newborn child was given an ear of corn at birth and endowed with a "corn name." An ear of maize was put in the place of death as the "heart of the deceased" and later used as seed corn to begin the cycle of life anew. To Navajos, corn is as sacred as human life.

— B. E. Johansen

SEE ALSO:
Agriculture, Native American; Deloria, Vine, Jr.; First Salmon Ceremony; Standing Bear, Luther; Turtle Island.

EDMO, ED (1946–)

Ed Edmo, born March 16, 1946, is a Shoshone/Bannock poet, actor, playwright, short story writer, traditional storyteller, and lecturer on Pacific Northwest tribal cultures.

Edmo lives in Portland, Oregon, and works throughout Oregon in the Artist in Education Programs, where he teaches poetry and creative writing and discusses Native American political issues with students of all ages in schools and colleges. He is a founding member of the Pacific Northwest Native American Writers Association, and he has won awards in Oregon for his plays. He also conducts workshops on various cultural issues and values for a wide range of groups, including youth, church, senior, civic, and human services personnel.

His books of poetry published in the United States include *Bridge of the Gods, Mountains of Fire* (San Francisco: Friends of the Earth, 1980) and *These Few Words of Mine* (Marvin, SD: The Blue Cloud Quarterly Press, 1985). He has also published a volume of poetry in New Zealand, *A Nation With-in* (Hamilton: Outrigger Press, 1983). His short fiction has been anthologized in *Talking Leaves: Contemporary Native American Short Stories* (New York: Laurel, 1991).

In 1992, he performed his one-man play, *Coyote*, at Returning the Gift, a weeklong conference that brought together nearly four hundred Native creative writers from throughout the upper Western Hemisphere. The participation of playwrights such as Edmo at Returning the Gift played an important role in the inauguration of the *Native Playwrights Newsletter*, which now chronicles the activities of Native theatrical companies throughout the North American continent and features in-depth interviews with leading Native playwrights.

SEE ALSO:
Returning the Gift.

EFFIGY

SEE Serpent Mound.

ELDERLY PEOPLE

When older people are no longer well enough to work and earn a living or are no longer able to live on their own, some people believe they are no longer useful to society and should live in retirement homes. Their care is seen as a burden to the family rather than a responsibility. This is not true in Native American communities.

Elderly people are and always have been an integral part of the life of the tribe. Different Indian nations have various stories, customs, and traditions, but common to all of them is the value they place on all life, and particularly on the lives of the older people of the community, the elders. There are presently 165,000 Native American elders age sixty-five or older in the United States. They comprise 8 percent of the American Indian–Alaska Native population, represent more than 50 percent of tribal groups nationwide, and speak 150 different languages. Eighty percent of these elders live west of the Mississippi River and are divided about evenly between urban and rural households.

The elders' role in traditional society, before disruption by European cultures, was as a stabilizing influence. They were the main source of religious, cultural, and social values, and they were respected not for their formal education but for their years of life experience. Part of this tradition of respect for elders was the result of a strong sense of the tribe as a community, with each member being dependent on the others. Everyone was valuable, and so everyone's actions should benefit the community.

Native American children are much more likely to grow up knowing the oldest generation of their people than are children in mainstream American culture, where the elderly are often placed in nursing homes.

In a large extended family, which might include uncles, aunts, grandchildren, and other relatives, elders served as teachers and counselors. The job of educating children was often turned over to an elderly uncle and it was not uncommon for grandparents to raise children while younger adults worked to provide for the family.

Elders are valued and honored in Native American societies for their traditional cultural knowledge, which is handed down in the form of stories. In the oral tradition, stories are the heart of the culture.

After the 1800s, life for elders changed dramatically. When the federal government made efforts to integrate Indians into the general population, many elders began to feel out of place. The knowledge they possessed and were responsible for passing on to the young was replaced by new ideas, new ways of living. Traditional medicines were replaced by more modern remedies. Traditional tribal leadership patterns were replaced by appointed or elected officials. Indian children were sent to special boarding schools and were no longer taught by the elders. As a result, many elders felt safer on the reservation, where there were still traditional lifeways, ceremonies, and language. Reservations, however, were often not rich in resources, and life on the reservation was hard. Many reservations struggled with poverty and hopelessness. Also, the connection between community members weakened as more and more children were educated by public schools and did not learn the old ways.

In 1976, trying to improve reservation life, Congress passed the Indian Health Care Improvement Act, which promised adequate care for all Indians. Despite this, Indian elders still have a life expectancy eight years less than the general population, and the 1980 U.S. Census found that 16 percent of them still lived without electricity or proper refrigeration, 50 percent had no telephone, and 26 percent had no indoor plumbing at all.

In 1986, the National Indian Council on Aging found that nearly one-half of the elderly had no heat but a woodburning stove or fireplace. Also, health care problems are sometimes extreme. Native Americans are 459 percent more likely to die of alcoholism, and diabetes among Indians is four times greater than the national average.

Despite the many health and social problems that continue to put a strain on family life for Native people, today's Native American communities do value their elders, and there are many programs trying to assist older people and improve their standard of living. In community centers and after-school programs, elders teach youngsters traditional dances and crafts. They also teach younger people old ways of believing and practical skills such as preparing traditional food and speaking the language of the tribe. For Cheyenne River Sioux, honoring and caring for the elderly are respected traditions. In Lakota, the word for "beautiful woman" metaphorically means "old woman." The Stillaguamish tribe (also known as Stoluckquamish) of northwestern Washington State has a program at its tribal center that pairs elders and children in order to teach the children the Lushootseed language. The Muscogee Nation has built one hundred housing units for older and physically disabled people, and many areas provide daily meals for elders.

Elders are still seen as the custodians of tribal history, culture, and lifeways, and tribal governments are working to ensure the transmission of traditional culture to younger generations. Elders understand the past and have the wisdom of experience.

— K. Broyles

SEE ALSO:
Children; Family, Role in Native Society.

ENCOMIENDA

The *encomienda* was a Spanish system of forced labor. It had its origins in the Spanish reconquest of the Iberian Peninsula (the Spanish homeland in Europe and the location of Spain and Portugal today). During the height of Muslim expansion during the Middle Ages, the Muslims had conquered Spain. For several generations after that, Spaniards were occupied in a war of religious fervor to regain political control of their homeland by driving the Muslims out of Spain. Muslims were not Christians and were therefore considered infidels (nonbelievers) by the fervently Catholic Spaniards. Those who were not driven out of Spain were subjected to Spanish demands for forced labor as the Spanish gradually reconquered the peninsula. This underlying justification for forced labor—the fact that someone's religion was different—would carry over to the Spanish colonies in the Western Hemisphere.

The Spanish completed the reconquest of the Iberian Peninsula at about the same time that Columbus sailed on his first voyage to the Caribbean islands in 1492. This generation of Spaniards, who would begin the conquest of the Americas, were products of their times. They were intolerant of religions different from their own partly because they had been engaged in a long struggle to regain their homeland from Muslims. In times of war, in every kind of nation, hatred for the enemy is inflamed at the expense of reason. If the Americas had been "discovered" under different circumstances, by Europeans who had not recently been locked in a long struggle with a people of a different religion, things might have been different in the Americas. As it happened, however, it was Spaniards of the late fifteenth century who came to the Americas, and they brought with them attitudes and characteristics that had propelled them through several successive generations of religious warfare.

Columbus established the first encomiendas in the Americas in 1498 when he returned to his base in the Caribbean, the town of Santo Domingo on the island of Hispaniola, and found his colony divided by a revolt led by Francisco Roldán. After attempting to defeat Roldán, Columbus was forced to negotiate a settlement with him. Roldán and others wanted a share of the wealth. To appease them, Columbus established encomiendas for individual Spaniards. Known as *encomenderos,* these individual Spaniards would hold a legal right to exact both tribute and labor from Native people. This practice would keep the encomenderos in the gentlemanly *hidalgo* status they sought and free them from the necessity of doing any manual labor. (Hidalgos were members of the minor Spanish nobility.)

In return for this position of privilege, and as the institution of the encomienda evolved and adapted to conditions in the Americas, the encomendero would be obligated to relieve the Spanish Crown of the responsibility for seeing that the Natives were instructed in the Christian religion, and, in theory, to be their protector. Each encomienda would encompass a specific group of Natives and would be hereditary, forming the basis for a Spanish family's wealth. Though not outright slavery as a fine point of Spanish law, it was not far from it and was at best a form of very crude feudalism. Native people soon found themselves at the mercy of the encomenderos.

Columbus extended the institution of the encomienda to the Americas without the blessings of the Spanish monarchy. The crown had explic-itly forbidden him to mistreat Native people, fearing it would hinder their conversion to Christianity, and Queen Isabella in particular had been furious with him when he had returned to Spain with five hundred Native slaves. Upon learning that they were being sold in the slave markets of Seville, she had ordered them freed and returned to their homes in the Americas. But the crown, despite grumblings and misgivings, yielded to circumstance and allowed the institution of the encomienda to persist, with Queen Isabella officially approving it as a temporary measure after Nicolás de Ovando became governor of Hispaniola in 1502 and pleaded with her that it was necessary. Once authorized by the crown, the encomienda soon spread along with the conquest of other islands, including Cuba in 1511, with devastating results for indigenous peoples. It was a decision the Spanish monarchy would regret, as encomenderos would prove to be a vexing problem for the crown. It would also be an institution the crown would have difficulty terminating.

The institution of the encomienda is an example of the great difference between the nature of the Spanish colonial experience in the Americas and that of other European colonial powers. To Spaniards, Native peoples themselves represented wealth, in the form of tribute and labor. Where the English might covet the land and view Native populations as a hindrance to their taking possession of it, and where the French might covet the furs of animals for their value in Europe and view trade with the Native populations as a means of acquiring furs, the Spaniards coveted the Native people themselves. Spaniards wanted their tribute, their labor, and their "souls." To the fervently Catholic Spaniards, tribute and labor were viewed as a fair price for indoctrinating the Native peoples of the Americas with European religious ideas. Rather than being exterminated or driven beyond the ever-spreading borders of colonization, Native peoples within the Spanish sphere of influence found themselves prisoners within their homelands, with their social, political, and religious institutions under full assault by the colonizers.

To their credit, learned Spaniards in the universities and at the royal court, as well as religious officials at all levels, debated the morality of institutions such as the encomienda and other matters regarding the nature, status, and rights of Native

This mural by Diego Rivera in the National Palace of Mexico City depicts the forced labor of Indians at the time Cortés arrived on the continent. Cortés was forbidden by the King of Spain from granting encomiendas for forced Indian labor in Mexico. He ignored the order.

peoples within the Spanish Empire. People such as Bartolomé de Las Casas arose, demanding more humane and just institutions. As will be seen, these concerns did not fall on deaf ears at the highest seats of power. Thousands of miles (kilometers) away, however, in the colonies, expediency—doing what seemed to best suit the interests of the colonists—proved to be too great an obstacle for meaningful reform to overcome. After about 1650, moral debate over the treatment of Indian people lessened considerably, and the encomienda became primarily a concern for the Spanish monarchy because the encomenderos presented a threat to royal power in the colonies.

Before reforms could even be contemplated, Native peoples were subjected to the merciless policies of Ferdinand II of Aragon, who encouraged slave raiding, from which he shared in the profits.

Many islands in the Bahamas were depopulated during this time. Everywhere the Spaniards went, Native populations declined drastically, by more than half in the first fifty years. European diseases for which the indigenous population had no immunities accounted for much of the loss, but so did slave raiding and brutal forced-labor conditions in mines. Enslaved Native populations died rapidly, creating a perpetual labor shortage. Before long, the Spanish began importing slaves from Africa into the islands.

Hernán Cortés, the Spanish explorer and conqueror of Mexico, was specifically forbidden to establish encomiendas in Mexico by Charles V. Cortés simply ignored the order. When Cortés left Mexico in 1527 and local Spanish politician Nuño de Guzmán seized power, Native peoples in Mexico were subjected to a period of severe abuse that rivaled the policies Ferdinand had implemented in the Caribbean.

Finally, in 1542, Charles V, in pronouncements known as the New Laws, decreed an immediate termination of the institution of the encomienda. When encomenderos in Peru learned of this, they revolted. When the new viceroy arrived in Peru to implement the New Laws, the encomenderos met his ship at the dock, disarmed the viceroy and his party, and forced them back aboard their ship. In order to put down the revolt, another new viceroy found it necessary to bribe some of the strongest encomenderos by bargaining with them so they would be allowed to retain their encomiendas.

Charles V found it expedient to approve this arrangement. Thereafter, however, having seen the threat to royal authority that the encomenderos posed, the crown took every opportunity to decrease their number, promulgating laws that made it easy for encomiendas to lapse, or pass on, to the state and difficult to be maintained and passed by inheritance. It took many generations, but by the eighteenth century nearly all of the large encomiendas had lapsed to the state. By 1720, the encomienda had been abolished everywhere except in Chile.

As the proportion of Indians subjugated to the encomienda grew smaller and the proportion characterized as state Indians increased, Indians found themselves little better off. State Indians became subject to an institution of forced labor that came to be known as the Cuatequil system, where they worked under the authority of an official known as a *corregidor*. Under this system, introduced in Peru in 1565, the Native peoples were to be subject to the demands of state labor four times a year, each time for a period of two weeks.

On paper, people were guaranteed many protections, including a wage and decent treatment. In operation, however, corregidores bought their positions from the viceroy until 1678, and afterward they bought their positions from the crown. The corregidores then attempted to make the most profit they could by maneuvering around the laws that had been intended to protect the Indians from excessive demands for forced labor, from little or no wages, and from inhumane treatment.

Other features of the Cuatequil system included the *mita*, which was a labor draft, and the *repar-* *timiento*, which forced Native peoples to purchase certain specified goods every two and one-half years from the corregidores. The repartimiento had been intended as a means of guaranteeing that Native peoples did not squander what little money they acquired and of ensuring that they should have necessary farm equipment. But it soon degenerated into an enterprise in which corregidores sold them shoddy, high-priced goods at great profit.

During the seventeenth and eighteenth centuries, Indians began falling under the system of debt peonage, in which their employers sold them necessities on credit, keeping them forever bound to jobs that paid very little and offered no future. Today, that system still plagues Native peoples throughout the Americas.

— D. L. Birchfield

SEE ALSO:

Christian Colonists' Views of Natives; Columbus, Christopher; Cortés, Hernán; Ferdinand and Isabella; Hispaniola; Las Casas, Bartolomé de; Spain.

SUGGESTED READINGS:

Bannon, John Francis. *The Spanish Borderlands Frontier: 1513–1821.* New York: Holt, Rinehart and Winston, 1970.

Fagg, John Edwin. *Latin America: A General History.* 2nd ed. New York: Macmillan, 1969.

Stoddard, Ellwyn R., et. al., eds. *Borderlands Sourcebook: A Guide to the Literature on Northern Mexico and the American Southwest.* Norman: University of Oklahoma Press, 1983.

ENGLAND

Early in the sixteenth century, the English began a period of continuous colonization of the Native homeland along the North American Atlantic coast. As English immigrants moved onto the land, they brought their language and culture, including their political and economic systems, and their diseases.

The first English to appear on the shores of North America were explorers and traders, including John Cabot (1497–1498), Sebastian Cabot (1509), Martin Frobisher (1576–1578), and Henry

These Indian men and women were painted by George Catlin in London. Native peoples excited great curiosity among the British whenever their representatives visited England.

Hudson (1609–1611). Hudson's North American voyage in 1609 was financed by the Dutch East Indian Company, a trading firm. Money for his 1610 expedition came from a group of English merchants. Like any of the trading companies, their goal was profit in trade goods.

The 1610 Hudson voyage was the basis for England's claim to the area surrounding Canada's vast inland sea, which would later be known as Hudson Bay. With this claim came more traders and more immigrants. Gradually, an extensive system of English trading posts was established in the Hudson Bay area, and in 1668, the first large-scale English commercial enterprise began at a trading post at the south end of the bay; this became the Hudson's Bay Company.

Trading posts did not exist in isolation, of course. Native people (Inuit and various Indian tribes) lived in communities along the river systems and inland on the tundra. The Native people already had an efficient, well-developed trading system— an economic infrastructure that was soon exploited by European traders. Natives quickly adapted to large-scale trading in animal pelts; beaver, fox, marten, wolverine, river otter, mink, and wolf were among the furs in greatest demand. Indians also manufactured and traded canoes and snowshoes. Without the Natives' skills and their hunting, fishing, and survival abilities, European endeavors would have been doomed.

But enterprising Natives in eastern Canada were so successful that the fur supply declined in the area, and the English shifted their objectives inland and westward. To the west was a whole new set of challenges and decisions for the English and the Natives.

Rivers and land routes that took the English to new fur sources were already dotted with French trading posts. By extending their struggle for economic power to North America, the French and English added to and created more opportunities for Native discord and intertribal warfare. Instead of uniting against the Europeans, tribes that were already long-time adversaries of one another formed alliances with the French and English.

Different tribes began interacting with each other along the lines of European conflicts or alliances. The powerful Iroquois nations (Mohawk, Seneca, Onondaga, Oneida, and Cayuga) sided with the English against the French, who were allied with the Iroquois's old enemies, the Algonquians. The Hurons were also allied with the French trappers. Part of the allegiance to the French was for economic reasons. Furthermore, while the English rarely adopted Native ways or married Natives, many French trappers did. From a tribal viewpoint, these in-laws were relatives. Thus, family interests were also at stake.

As each European nation prepared to back its North American claims, Natives focused on protecting their homelands. The stage was set for a showdown. The resulting series of armed conflicts lasted from 1689 to 1763. There were actually four wars in all during this time. Probably the best known of these was the final one—the Seven Years' War (referred to by Britain as the French and Indian War). By 1763, much of the area east of the Mississippi River (from Florida north to Canada, especially along the St. Lawrence Seaway) had been affected by the war. Victory came to England in the French and Indian War. Then attention turned toward conflicts between England and its colonies, as well as conflicts among the colonies themselves. Both in Europe and North America, the English quickly lost interest in their former allies among Native tribes. As the colonists gradually moved toward independence from England, first as a confederacy, then later as a union with a constitution, tides of immigrants moved westward. Hundreds of Native cultures fell victim to the immigrants' insatiable need for land.

For the colonists, as for the Natives, strength rested in unity. Ironically, it was the Iroquois Confederacy and constitution that provided a well-developed model for the colonies. Iroquois leaders attended the meeting in Albany, New York, when Benjamin Franklin proposed the Plan of Union. As he pleaded for political unification of the thirteen colonies, Franklin referred to the Iroquois government: "It would be a strange thing if Six Nations of ignorant savages should be capable of forming a scheme for such a union, and be able to execute it in such a manner that it has subsisted for ages and appears indissoluble; and yet that a like union should be impracticable for ten or a dozen English colonies, to whom it is more necessary and must be more advantageous, and who cannot be supposed to want an equal understanding of their interest."

The Native nations to which Franklin referred were ust as diverse in their cultures and languages as were the thirteen colonies. Although colonists were conscious of their own differences in religion, customs, and language, they rarely noticed differences among Native American nations. Natives, in contrast, were keenly aware of diversity among the colonies, especially among the English with their sharply contrasting customs and religions.

It would have been difficult for even a European to believe that the 1600s Hudson's Bay traders and the Massachusetts Bay Puritans came from the same nation. They differed in dress, in the way they lived and governed themselves, and in the way they interacted with Natives. Likewise, Puritans differed from the Quakers, the Shakers, and the many other English immigrants who had come to "discover" and change the "New World."

The colonists' ill-founded determination to "civilize" Natives was clearly summed up by the Chief of the Senecas, Sagoyewatha (Red Jacket), in a council speech given in Buffalo, New York, in 1805. In reply to a missionary seeking permission to convert northern New York State Natives, Sagoyewatha said:

Brother, continue to listen. You say that you are sent to instruct us how to worship the Great Spirit agreeably to his mind, and if we do not take hold of the religion which you white people teach, we shall be unhappy hereafter; you say that you are right, and we are lost; how do we know this to be true? We understand that your religion is written in a book; if it was intended for us as well as you, why has not the Great Spirit given it to us, and not only to us, but why did he not give to our forefathers the knowledge of that book, with the means of understanding it rightly? We only know what you tell us about it; how shall we know when to believe, being so often deceived by the white people?

Brother, you say there is but one way to worship and serve the Great Spirit; if there is but one religion, why do you white people differ so much about it? Why not all agree, as you can all read the book?

Brother, we do not understand these things; we are told that your religion was given to your forefathers, and has been handed down from father to son. We also have a religion which was given to our forefathers, and has been handed down to us their children. We worship that way. It teacheth us to be thankful for all the favors we receive; to love each other, and to be united; we never quarrel about religion.

Sagoyewatha's speech in its entirety presents a vivid picture of English–Native American contradictions and interactions, a recollection of the past and a vision of the future. Sagoyewatha recalled the landing of the Pilgrims, "Their members were small; they found friends, and not enemies. . . . At length, their numbers had greatly increased; they wanted more land . . . war took place; Indians were hired to fight against Indians . . . they also brought strong liquors among us; it was strong and powerful and has slain thousands."

This story would be repeated again and again. Scenes, dates, and events changed. Voices of other great chiefs and orators would be heard.

As the colonists fought English troops during the American Revolutionary War, Natives again allied themselves with one faction or the other. Few remained neutral. For some it was almost like a civil war: Algonquians in Massachusetts helped the colonists, while west of the Appalachian Mountains, other Algonquians helped the English, hoping to block the tide of expansion into Native land.

Victory came to the revolutionary colonists and their allies. But again, Native allies were denied their share of benefits. No matter which side a tribe had fought for during the Revolution, they and their lands were swamped by the settlers' westward expansion. Tribes that had backed the colonists

suffered, just as did those, such as the Tennessee Cherokees, who had backed England.

In the early years of the 1800s, the new government of the United States purchased from France title to vast lands west of the Mississippi, known as the Louisiana Purchase. The United States also gained title to lands from Spain. These purchases roughly doubled the size of the new nation.

Growth of the United States and its rising political power were opposed by England, eventually triggering the War of 1812. Once again, the pattern of Native alliance and betrayal was repeated. Among the tribes allied with England were the Shawnees and a faction of the Creeks. Shawnee leader Tecumseh, appointed brigadier general by the English, led a force of two thousand warriors. Tecumseh, along with his brother, The Prophet, tried to persuade southeastern tribes to join tribes of the Ohio River Valley in a confederacy that would hold their lands against invasion by citizens of the United States. Again, England lost its war, as did Tecumseh and his followers.

After the War of 1812, conflicts between England and the United States were fought with economic and diplomatic weapons. English influences in North America remained strong for the next century, affecting both Natives and the "new" Americans.

As Native American homelands were systematically invaded, Native survivors were pressured to give up their religions, their languages, and their cultures. By the end of the nineteenth century, Native children were taken from their families and sent to schools, usually at great distances from their homes. These schools were based on the English system of education, and many of the texts were published in England. Native people became subject to United States law, based on the English system. Tribal courts and tribal governments were disbanded.

Forced assimilation was not as apparent in Canada, although Canada was under direct English rule as a commonwealth (political unit) of England. Initially, Canada's Native nations were not as hard-pressed as their southern neighbors. The northern lands were vast, with few railroads into Native reserves and less immigration by Europeans. These factors plus the mediation between Natives

This photo shows Os-ke-non-ton, a Mohawk singer, visiting the grave of William Penn, one of the founding colonizers of Pennsylvania, in England in 1928.

U.S. Army across hundreds of miles (kilometers) of mountains, from Idaho through Lolo Pass into Montana, down the Bitterroot Valley, then up the Flathead. The Nez Perces were within forty miles (sixty-four kilometers) of Canada before injuries, exhaustion, and starvation broke their drive long enough for the army to catch up and surround them with overwhelming odds.

Nearly five hundred years of contact between the peoples of England and North America have profoundly altered both. Diseases and weapons from Europe have killed millions of Natives. Their cultures have been ravaged and their homelands stolen. Yet, most tribes survive. And beyond survival, they have given the world concepts of personal freedom and dignity and of government that limits the power of officials to tyrannize.

— J. Arteno

and the English by the Northwest Mounted Police provided a less negative experience for both.

In fact, many historians consider mediation by the Mounties to have been the major factor for the relative peacefulness between the two groups. Contrary to the U.S. Army approach, the Mounties focused on specific individuals and groups, including non-Natives. Mountie authority and success came from personal relations developed with Natives by these men in traditional scarlet English jackets.

Canada sometimes became a haven for Natives struggling for survival against the U. S. Cavalry. Perhaps most famous of the tribes that sought refuge in Canada were the Sioux led by Sitting Bull and the Nez Perces led by Chief Joseph. The Nez Perces fought a running battle against several corps of the

SEE ALSO:

Albany Plan of Union; Canada, Native–Non-Native Relations in; European Attitudes Toward Indigenous Peoples; Iroquois Confederacy; Tecumseh.

SUGGESTED READINGS:

Debo, Angie. *A History of the Indians of the United States*. Norman: University of Oklahoma Press, 1970.

Dickason, Olive Patricia. *Canada's First Nations: A History of Founding Peoples from Earliest Times*. Norman: University of Oklahoma Press, 1992.

Forbes, Jack D. *Columbus and Other Cannibals*. New York: Autonomedia, 1992.

Todorov, Tzvetan. *The Conquest of America*. Translated by Richard Howard. New York: Harper and Row, 1984.

Willison, George F. *The Pilgrim Reader*. New York: Doubleday, 1953.

EN'OWKIN CENTRE

The En'owkin (pronounced en-OW-kin) Centre is an internationally recognized First Nations, or Native, training center located in Penticton, British Columbia, Canada. It was established in 1981 by the six First Nations bands that form the Okanagan Tribal Council and is affiliated with the University of Victoria. Although the Centre is governed by the Okanagan Indian Educational Resources Society, a twelve-member board of directors is responsible for the organization's decision-making and policy development. Members of the board of directors serve from throughout North America and include such well-known authors as Creek poet Joy Harjo, originally from Oklahoma, who is a professor at the University of New Mexico. All of the teachers and support staff at the En'owkin Centre are of First Nations ancestry and include some of the leading Native writers of Canada, including Okanagan novelist Jeannette Armstrong (author of the novel *Slash* and editor of the anthology *Looking at the Words of Our People: First Nations Analysis of Literature*); Cree poet Beth Cuthand (author of *Horse Dance to Emerald Mountain* and *Voices in the Waterfall*); and science fiction writer Gerry William, a member of the Spallumcheen Indian Band (and author of *The Black Ship: Book One of Enid Blue Starbreaks*).

The Centre offers education and training for Native students in a number of areas: adult basic education, college achievement, Okanagan languages and linguistics, visual arts, and the international school of writing. The adult basic program is for students who wish to upgrade their education. The college achievement program prepares students for success in higher postsecondary education. The Okanagan languages and linguistics program earns students a certificate of Okanagan languages training. Visual arts is designed to develop and refine visual creativity. The International School of Writing is designed for First Nations students to find their voice as writers and to encourage them to interpret and record First Nations experiences. Students work with established First Nations writers and teachers.

The En'owkin Centre also is responsible for Theytus Books, a First Nations publishing company that publishes works by First Nations writers.

Theytus is an Okanagan term meaning "preserving by handing down." Theytus Books and the En'owkin Centre publish an annual anthology, entitled *Gatherings*, which features creative work by Native literary writers from throughout North America.

Staff and faculty from the En'owkin Centre and Theytus Books contributed significantly to the July 1992 weeklong gathering of nearly four hundred Native literary writers from throughout the upper Western Hemisphere, called Returning the Gift: A Festival of North American Native Writers, at the University of Oklahoma. The conference required years of planning and nearly three hundred thousand dollars in foundation grants and was a historic event for Native literature. At this conference, the Native Writers' Circle of the Americas was founded, as was Wordcraft Circle of Native Writers and Storytellers and the *Native Playwrights Newsletter*. Also, a number of anthologies were published as a result of it, including the *Returning the Gift* anthology, the *Neon Powwow* anthology, and anthologies of Navajo and Cherokee writers. Jeannette Armstrong, director of the En'owkin Centre, and Greg Young-Ing (Cree), managing editor of Theytus Books, gave plenary session speeches at the festival, and Armstrong served on the festival steering committee. Representatives of the En'owkin Centre also attended the Returning the Gift regional conferences in 1993 (Southwest, again at the University of Oklahoma), 1994 (Pacific Northwest, at Neah Bay, Washington, on the Makah Reservation), and 1995 (Midwest, at Green Bay, Wisconsin). The En'owkin Centre is host to the fifth annual Returning the Gift conference in the fall of 1996.

SEE ALSO:
Harjo, Joy; Returning the Gift.

ENROLLED INDIANS

Enrollment means membership in a tribe. Generally, Indian people who are enrolled are those who have met specific qualifications to be recognized as Indians. This may be recognition only by a tribe, by recognition of the members of one tribe by another tribe, or it may be recognition by a state or by the United States government.

As sovereign nations, tribes have the authority to accept individuals onto their roll of members. Acceptance usually means that the person must meet specific requirements. These requirements vary widely from tribe to tribe, and tribal rolls may be open (accepting new members) or closed (not accepting new members). As an example, to join a tribe, a person may have to be directly descended from a tribal member of full or half Indian blood, be able to speak the tribal language, and live on Indian land. In another tribe, one might only have to prove direct descent from a person who was officially listed on a United States government census of that tribe from a particular historical date. For many tribes in Oklahoma, one must be able to trace descent from the Dawes Commission allotment rolls. Since a number of people in each tribe opposed the allotment of their land and refused to be enrolled by the Dawes Commission, some full-blood Indians in the state are not enrolled.

The most important qualification to be on a roll approved by the federal government is usually family descent from persons officially listed on a census of tribal members collected by the United States government. According to the 1990 U.S. Census, there are almost two million recognized (enrolled) Indians in the United States. Of this number, less than half live on reservations, while more than half of all Indians in the United States live in urban areas.

SEE ALSO:
Dawes Commission; General Allotment Act.

ENTERTAINMENT AND THE PERFORMING ARTS

A great number of American Indians are involved in the rapidly expanding fields of the entertainment industry and the performing arts. For centuries, Native people have placed a high value on the performing arts. Performing arts such as storytelling, dancing, singing, and playing musical instruments continue to be a rich tradition, whether used for entertainment, celebration, or ceremony. And new American Indian artists are emerging all the time in disciplines such as live theater, music, dance, and cinema.

Mohawk actor Jay Silverheels as Tonto, sidekick of the Lone Ranger, became a television icon known to millions. Native Americans remember him for his humanitarian work on behalf of Indian people.

Oneida actor Graham Greene *(right)* learned his skills in the theater. He gained international fame opposite Kevin Costner *(left)* in the movie *Dances with Wolves.*

The first professional American Indian theater company in the United States, founded in the 1970s in New York City, was the Native American Theatre Ensemble. This ensemble paved the way for several other Indian theaters across the country. Among these are Red Eagle Soaring in Seattle, Spiderwoman Theatre in New York, the American Indian Theater Company in Tulsa, and the Indian Time Theater Company at Niagara Falls. Native theater has provided an arena for many talented artists and performers, such as Oneida actor and stand-up comedian Charles Hill; Aleut actress, director, and choreographer Jane Lind; Cree playwright Tomson Highway; Kiowa-Delaware playwright, director, and teacher Hanay Geiogamah; and Assiniboine playwright and teacher William S. Yellowrobe, Jr.

Native American performers in the film industry have probably had the broadest exposure. Will Rogers, a Cherokee from Oklahoma, became a national personality and celebrity in the earliest days of film. He made more than seventy motion pictures and also wrote six books and a column that appeared in 350 newspapers across the nation. Before his death in 1935, he was the highest-paid film and radio personality in the country.

Jay Silverheels (1912–1980), famous for his role as Tonto in *The Lone Ranger* television series, was a Mohawk from Canada. He was the first American Indian to have his star placed in Hollywood's Walk of Fame. Chief Dan George (1899–1981), a Squamish actor, received the New York Drama Critics Award in 1970 for his portrayal of Old Lodge Skins in the film *Little Big Man.* Creek actor Will Sampson (1934–1987) received an Academy Award nomination for his role as Chief Bromden in *One Flew Over the Cuckoo's Nest.*

Among the Native film actors working today is Tantoo Cardinal, a Cree-Métis and an award-winning actress from Canada who is perhaps best known for her supporting role in the 1991 movie *Dances with Wolves.* Oneida television and screen actor Graham Greene has appeared in a number of television series as well as in the films *Dances with*

485

Inuit-Cree actress Irene Bedard as Mary Crow Dog in the 1994 Turner Network Television production "Lakota Woman: Siege at Wounded Knee."

Wolves and *Thunderheart*. Wes Studi, a Cherokee actor, has performed in such popular movies as *Geronimo* and *The Last of the Mohicans*. Inuit-Cree actress Irene Bedard starred in the television film "Lakota Woman" and also provided the voice of Pocahontas in Disney's 1995 animated film of the same name. Cayuse-Nez Perce actress Elaine Miles played Marilyn on the Emmy Award–winning television series *Northern Exposure*.

Dance is another performing art to which Native Americans have made significant contributions. Five Native American women, all from Oklahoma, have soared as internationally famous ballerinas. Osage dancer Maria Tallchief performed with the Ballet Russe de Monte Carlo from 1942 to 1947, later becoming a leading ballerina with the New York City Ballet. Her sister, Majorie Tallchief, danced with the Grand Ballet du Marquis de Cuevas from 1947 to 1956. Roselle Hightower (Choctaw), Moscelyne Larkin (Shawnee-Peoria), and Yvonne Chouteau (Cherokee) also have gained worldwide prestige as ballerinas.

Some Native Americans have combined contemporary dance concepts and ancestral Indian dance to create vital and innovative choreography. Blackfeet-Ojibwe dancer Rosalie Jones, who founded the dance company Daystar in 1980, studied both traditional Indian and contemporary European dance steps and developed three dance productions that combined the forms. Rene Highway (1954–1990) was a Cree modern dance performer, teacher, and choreographer. Juan Valenzuela (1919–1986), a Spanish-Aztec-Yaqui, was a dancer and teacher committed to the promotion of modern dance within Indian communities. Belinda James, a Pueblo, is a classically trained dancer and choreographer who has been performing in New York City since the early 1980s.

Among the most notable Native American musical entertainers is Quapaw-Cherokee composer

Osage sisters Marjorie *(wearing hat)* and Maria Tallchief became international ballet stars.

Louis W. Ballard, who was nominated in 1972 for the Pulitzer Prize in music for his cantata *Portrait of Will Rogers*. Navajo-Ute flutist R. Carlos Nakai combines Sioux and Zuni melodies with contemporary elements. He has released a number of recordings.

World-famous opera star Bonnie Jo Hunt, a Sioux, sang with the San Francisco Opera and later led a program called Artists of Indian America, a group that conducts workshops and performances. Buffy Sainte-Marie, a Cree singer and songwriter, performs internationally; her songs are directly influenced by her Native American heritage.

Floyd Westerman, a Sioux folk singer and musician, toured college campuses in the 1970s. His first album, released in 1970, was called *Custer Died for Your Sins*. In addition to solo artists, there are also many Indian rock groups, country-and-western groups, and gospel groups.

Some of the fastest-rising Native artists are those involved in the music industry. Stockbridge-Mahican composer Brent Michael Davids (1960–) was commissioned by the Joffrey Ballet for *Moon of the Falling Leaves* (1992) and commissioned by the Kronos Quartet for two works, *The Singing Woods* (1994) and *The Turtle People* (1995). Davids is one of the few classically trained Native composers working today.

Cree singer Buffy Sainte-Marie in London in 1971 at the beginning of a three-week tour of Britain and Scandinavia. At the time, she had funded scholarships that had already put five Indian students through college.

Another rising star is Cherokee rapper and actor Litefoot. Litefoot has released three recordings on his own label, Red Vinyl Records: *The Money* (1992), *Native Tongue* (1993), and *Seein' Red* (1994). He also played a key role in Disney's *The Indian in the Cupboard* (1995).

— T. Midge

EPIDEMIC DISEASES

From the beginning of European exploration of the Americas, encounters between two radically different cultures—European and Native American— would have many profound and often devastating effects on Native people. In addition to the cultural, military, social, and economic changes that American Indians have withstood since European contact, they also suffered through medical problems brought on by exposure to certain diseases common in Europe but unkown in America until 1492. That is when Christopher Columbus and ninety Spaniards—whose ethnic origins have been traced back to the ancient Iberians, Phoenicians, Carthaginians, Romans, Vandals, Visigoths, and North African Muslims—landed on their shores. The Natives had no natural protection against the diseases brought by Columbus and his crew. (Except for the llama in the South American Andes, the Natives kept no domesticated livestock—the source of many human diseases, such as smallpox from cowpox and measles from the virus that causes rinderpest in cattle.) Within fifty years of their arrival, the Spaniards had conquered mighty civilizations and taken over huge areas of land. Much of their so-called success can be attributed to the diseases they brought.

Estimates of the pre-Columbian Native population throughout the Americas have ranged from 8.4 to 112 million, and 54 million is the widely accepted figure. As a result of Columbus's arrival, the Native population of America decreased by at least 90 percent.

Records kept by the Spaniards when they landed on the island of Hispaniola tell us that the population there was estimated at between 100,000 and 3 million people. Only 240 Natives were left alive forty-eight years later. When Cortés landed in Mexico in 1519, Native people numbered

Christopher Columbus attends a Christian ceremony in the Caribbean. Such early encounters would produce unfortunate consequences for Native people throughout the Americas. Epidemic diseases spread rapidly through the islands of the Caribbean and across the North American mainland, far ahead of the actual movement of the frontiers of European settlement.

between 5 and 25 million. In 1605, there were only 1 million left.

From 1617 to 1620, an epidemic devastated the Native population of Massachusetts Bay, opening the way for the arrival of the Pilgrims in 1620. For the next three centuries, the Indian people were wiped out by waves of epidemics to which they had no resistance. Smallpox, cholera, malaria, measles, swine influenza, and venereal diseases were introduced accidentally—and sometimes by design.

Some European colonizers considered the epidemics to be "divine providence"and "manifest destiny." In 1620, the royal patent for the Plymouth colony declared that "within this late yeares there hath by God's Visitation raigned a Wonderful Plague, to the utter Destruction, Devastation and Depopulation of the whole Territorye. Whereby We in our Judgement are persuaded and satisfied that the appointed Time is come in which the Almighty God in his great Goodness and Bountie towards Us and our People hath thought fitt and determined that those large and goodly Territoryes, deserted as it were by their naturall inhabitants should be possessed and enjoyed."

Although the numbers range from 800,000 to 30 million, most studies conclude that there were 5 million Native people living within the continental United States prior to European contact. By 1900, the physically battered Indians had been decimated to 237,000. Nearly all of the Native fatalities were caused by disease.

Prior to European contact, the Indian population was exceptionally healthy, except for some arthritis, bone tumors, parasites, and minor germs. The people generally lived a healthy lifestyle in uncrowded villages. They were knowledgeable about a large variety of native medicinal plants, and some of the Native cultures had impressive surgical skills.

Many Indians died of European diseases without ever seeing a European. As the Europeans advanced into the Americas, they entered regions already emptied by disease. One tragic example is the 1837 smallpox episode among the Mandans, a Plains nation. Days after a riverboat carrying people infected with smallpox landed in Mandan territory, tribal members fell victim to the disease. Within a few months, 1,870 had died, leaving only 130 alive.

The specter of smallpox was a frightening probability for all of the Indian tribes. In their winter count (a historical recording of each year), the Great Sioux Nation recorded the years 1818, 1845, and 1850 as "Smallpox." Other diseases, such as malaria, which originated in Africa and came to America with the slave trade, and yellow fever, another tropical disease, also had tragic health consequences for the Indian people.

Today, the health needs of American Indians continue to be very grave. As a group, Indians are a disadvantaged minority, lagging behind the general U.S. society in income, health, and other socioeconomic indicators. Poor health is strongly related to poverty in all segments of U.S. society. In the case of Native people, poor health and the susceptibility to certain medical ailments have been a fact of life since earliest contact with non-Native cultures, and poverty has only compounded the problem.

The Indian Health Service (IHS) is the primary source of health care services for most American Indians and Alaska Natives. The IHS and tribes operate 50 hospitals and 455 outpatient facilities. In spite of real improvements in health status among populations served by IHS during the last twenty-five years, death and disease rates for Indians are among the highest in the nation. Among the medical conditions that have affected Native people in disproportionately high numbers are tuberculosis, alcohol mortality, fetal alcohol syndrome, diabetes, and, in more recent years, AIDS and HIV disease. Also, the rate of attempted suicide among Indian adolescents is four times that of other teens.

Changes wrought by the dominant society are also placing the Native population at risk. Pesticides and other toxic pollutants are affecting the health of as many as 85 to 90 percent of American Indians, resulting in chronic fatigue syndrome (CFS), multiple chemical sensitivity (MCS), and other related disease complexes. Besides causing poor health and disability, another chilling effect of pollutants on American Indians is the high numbers of miscarriages, stillborns, and low-birth-weight babies among those affected.

— T. Hansen

SEE ALSO:

AIDS; Alcoholism; Children; Columbian Exchange; Demography, Native; Fetal Alcohol Syndrome; Indian Health Service; Manifest Destiny; Smallpox.

ERDRICH, LOUISE (1954–)

Louise Erdrich, a Turtle Mountain Chippewa (Ojibwe), was born in Little Falls, North Dakota, and attended schools in Wahpeton, North Dakota. After Erdrich graduated from Dartmouth in 1976 with a degree in creative writing and from Johns Hopkins with a master's, she published her first book of poems, *Jacklight*, in 1984. The poems serve as a companion piece to Erdrich's novel *Love Medicine* in that many similar characters appear in the novel that remind readers of those in the poems.

Love Medicine is one of the most highly awarded novels in recent decades, named the best work of fiction of 1984 by the National Book Critics Circle, among other accolades. The characters in *Love Medicine* and *Jacklight* discover startling connections that bind them together and make them think about the complications of kinship. In *Love Medicine*, there is an emphasis on spiritual ties over biological ones.

Love Medicine is the first novel in Erdrich's tetralogy, her four books that form a series, which contains recurring characters whose homes are around Turtle Mountain reservation and other places in the Midwest. The three other books are *Tracks* (1988), *The Beet Queen* (1986), and *The Bingo Palace* (1994). *Tracks* concerns the generations before *Love Medicine*, who are struggling to retain their land base, which is being stolen from them by the encroaching United States government; *The Beet Queen* explores the German side of Erdrich's heritage; and *The Bingo Palace* pulls everything together—previous generations and present-day relatives, white and Indian.

At her best, the strength of Erdrich's writing lies in her ability to create characters who sound convincing and yet speak lyrically at the same time. Erdrich's second book of poetry, *Baptism of Desire*, published in 1989, like *Jacklight*, provides an interesting comparison to characters throughout the tetralogy. Very recently, Erdrich has published a new and expanded version of *Love Medicine*, basing the new work on the assumption that in an oral tradition, stories are always evolving over time as tellers adapt their tellings to new audiences and changing experiences.

SEE ALSO:
Dorris, Michael.

ETHNOGRAPHY

Ethnography is the description of a society or culture that comes from living among a group of people and taking part in many of their activities while observing and recording as much as possible of what occurs. This technique, called participant observation, is a part of the firsthand fieldwork that ethnographers conduct in their study of a community.

Many people confuse *ethnography* with *ethnology*. The purpose of *ethnography* is mainly to participate, observe, and record the life of a culture and to produce a description of that culture based on the recorded observations. The purpose of *ethnology* is more scientific or theoretical. Ethnologists compare the results of ethnographic observations of more than one culture. They then form theories or generalizations about those cultures based on the information they have gathered. Ethnology thus uses ethnography as a principal way of gathering information in its study of a culture.

Ethnographic work involves every area of anthropology—linguistics, archaeology, analysis of traditional stories, collection of folklore and medicine, and many other studies. Much cultural information in the United States began to be gathered starting in the 1880s with the formation of the Bureau of American Ethnology. The Bureau published two series, its *Annual Reports* and *Annual Bulletins*, as its main publications, though lesser series were also printed. Eighty-one *Annual Reports* were published and 193 *Annual Bulletins* between 1879 and 1964, when the bureau was merged with the Department of Anthropology, United States National Museum, to form the Smithsonian Office of Anthropology.

Though the bureau amassed a huge body of information of tremendous historical worth, the manner in which it represented the information and its reasons for recording it are highly controversial among Indian people. The fact that the first head of the bureau, John Wesley Powell, was a major in the U.S. Army, suggests that the information gathered from Native people was to be used for military purposes. And some historians also feel that the fact that the bureau's origins are tied to the U.S. Geological Survey reflects an attitude that Indians were valued more as nonhumans—like layers of rock—than as members of existing cultures.

In addition to using archaeological and other physical evidence, ethnographers also try to represent Native literatures and cultures through writings based on information gathered from Natives and Native works. One large area of ethnographic work is translation.

One of the problems faced by translators doing ethnographic work is whether to render a more *literal* or *literary* translation. A *literal* translation, though relatively accurate, is usually very difficult for non-Native readers to understand. Sentences in Native languages have completely different word orders than in English, and sentences rendered literally would produce a jigsaw puzzle for the reader to try to piece together. A more *literary* translation reproduces the words of the story, song, or chant in an order familiar to Western ears, requiring greater manipulation of the original language on the part of the translator.

In addition to these concerns, the translator must consider the cultural contexts, or settings, that are lost in translation. In oral communities, the audiences already know much background information for the stories since they have seen them performed in ritual and ceremony. An appreciation of how much listeners already know can be quickly gained by even a brief glance at Paul Radin's Winnebago trickster stories in his book *The Trickster: A Study in American Indian Mythology.* Radin's book contains many footnotes. These footnotes, which make up a text that is almost as large as the stories themselves, are full of background information. The footnotes explain cultural facts to readers that Winnebago listeners would have already known.

A very early attempt at translation was Henry Rowe Schoolcraft's work with Ojibwe (Chippewa) song and chant. It was upon this work that Henry Wadsworth Longfellow based his poem "Hiawatha." Schoolcraft rendered the Ojibwe material in rhymed and metered verse that yielded poor translations, yet he did offer, in some cases, more literal, word-for-word translations as well.

In the last twenty years, the work of three scholars, Dennis Tedlock, Dell Hymes, and Jerome Rothenberg, has become prominent in the field of translation. Dennis Tedlock, in his 1972 pioneer work *Finding the Center: Narrative Poetry of the Zuni Indians,* attempts to recapture the experience of an oral performance for a reader in the same way that it occurs for the listener. This is a goal of Hymes and Rothenberg as well. All three men seem to be

Spokane–Coeur d'Alene writer Sherman Alexie signs copies of his books. Alexie, who not so much reads as performs from his writings, exemplifies the oral tradition at work in Native cultures.

influenced by modern poetry, which, when read aloud, uses breath and the rhythms of the performer's breathing, rather than word "pictures," to create its effect on both performer and audience. For example, Tedlock's renderings of stories might be compared to a musical score in which he uses different types of print to represent sound. If a storyteller raises her voice, for instance, Tedlock uses boldface or larger letters. One problem with this way of representing sound is that Tedlock's uses of type become so complicated that they clutter up the page and distract the reader rather than enhance the story, sometimes requiring detailed explanations as to what all the typography means. The stories do not always stand well on their own without an explanation by the translator.

While Tedlock must work with tape recordings since he is interested in representing sound variations, Dell Hymes works with texts for which there are only written records. Hymes takes old written versions of Northwestern Native languages that were previously represented in a prose format and breaks them into lines, making them look like poetry. Based on his understanding of storytelling techniques, he uses the line breaks to give an idea of the storyteller's pauses in the original oral performance. Of course, the reader has no way of knowing how close the written version comes to the oral one.

Laguna novelist and poet Leslie Silko, like many other Native writers, very often breaks up stories into poetic lines, much as Hymes does, and, presumably, to create the same effect, the simulation of a storytelling voice. This is not to suggest that Native writers got the idea from Hymes necessarily but to point out a similar quest for a means to represent oral stories.

Jerome Rothenberg's translations of Native stories in *Shaking the Pumpkin: Traditional Poetry of the Indian North Americas* are what he calls "translations of translations" that that have already been made in English. In these translations of translations, Rothenberg is less concerned with giving an accurate translation of an original story than he is with re-creating the feeling of a storytelling performance. Though Rothenberg's versions are often powerful and moving, he has sometimes been criticized for going so far afield from the original culture as to become unfaithful to the tradition within which he is working.

Each of these three translators has his strong and weak points, but every translation is a representation, or an impression, of an oral performance, and not the actual performance. It is impossible for the reading audience to experience the story the same way as the listening audience hears it because communal cultures affected by the oral tradition see the world differently and perceive the story shaped by their worldviews—just as readers, whose perception is based on books, newspapers, computer screens, and other visual media, see the story as it is shaped by *their* worldview.

— C. S. Womack

SEE ALSO:
Bureau of American Ethnology; Storytelling.

SUGGESTED READINGS:
Hymes, Dell. *"In Vain I Tried to Tell You": Essays in Native American Ethnopoetics*. Philadelphia: University of Pennsylvania Press, 1981.

Krupat, Arnold. *Ethnocriticism: Ethnography, History, Literature*. Berkeley: University of California Press, 1992.

Rothenberg, Jerome. *Shaking the Pumpkin: Traditional Poetry of the Indian North Americas*. Garden City, NY: Doubleday, 1972.

Swann, Brian. *On the Translation of Native American Literatures*. Washington, D.C.: Smithsonian Institution Press, 1992.

Tedlock, Dennis. *The Spoken Word and the Work of Interpretation*. Philadelphia: University of Pennsylvania Press, 1983.

EUROPEAN-AMERICANS

Within decades of the first landfall by Spanish sailors under the command of Christopher Columbus over five hundred years ago, Europeans have dominated North America politically, culturally, and technologically. Seeking to transplant their "old-world" customs and ideas into the "new world" that America represented to them, transplanted European explorers, conquerors, missionaries, and settlers came for a variety of reasons. They came from countries where landownership defined prosperity and class. They came looking for new mar-

A depiction of Columbus at Isla Margarita in the Caribbean. Beginning with Columbus, Europeans would strive for many generations to learn the nature of the lands of the Western Hemisphere. Few of them, however, would seek to know and appreciate the indigenous cultures of those lands.

kets. They came looking for religious freedom. Above all, they came looking for wealth. However clear their reasons for coming to America may have been, the attitudes of Europeans toward the Native American peoples, the original occupants of North America, have not always been so clear, often providing a study in contrast and confusion.

Throughout the history of contact between European and Native cultures, Euro-Americans have often shown little consistency in their perceptions or policies regarding Native Americans. Rather, Indian policy often appears to have been based primarily upon ignorance, greed, and political expediency. European-American attitudes have likewise seemed inconsistent, although they have usually been steeped in a variety of convenient stereotypes about Native Americans. These stereotypes have remained strong and have often dictated public opinion about Native Americans. Often, these stereotypes have informed U.S. policy decisions regarding the original Americans.

One persistent stereotype is that of the Indian as the "vanishing American." The image of Native Americans hovering on the brink of extinction due to the combined forces of disease, alcohol, warfare, and loss of land was eagerly seized upon by Euro-Americans as an inevitable fate for Native America in the eighteenth century, and it lingers to this day. This belief led European-Americans to study Indians as curiosities, as objects suited for museums. It may even have rationalized such misguided and vicious efforts as removal, in order to "preserve" remaining Indians on reservations, in isolation from European-Americans. In spite of the deep losses suffered by Native Americans, they continue to persist as small but robust cultures in the modern world.

One generalization that has been promoted in European-American popular culture is that "Indian" refers to a single tribe, a single people, a single culture. This belief fails to recognize the differences—cultural, philosophical, and linguistic—among some five hundred different nations of people occupying North America. This mistaken view has led to the convenience of treating all Native Americans alike in many different arenas—political, educational, social, and governmental—often with devastating results. It has prevented Euro-Americans from really learning about or knowing Native Americans as people.

The view of the Indian as an "ignorant savage" is familiar to those who have seen old Western movies. This popular belief was rampant during nineteenth-century European-American westward expansion, and it helped to justify the hostilities practiced by U.S. military and civilian alike against Native Americans who occupied the land desired by the European-Americans.

A current stereotype popularized in the latter part of the twentieth century involves the resurrection of an old favorite: "the Noble Savage." This belief romanticizes Native American lifestyles and traditional values, and it has led to a wholesale adoption of Native American spiritual practices, out of context, by some European-Americans—a practice that is offensive to most Indian people, who see it as disrespectful of Native cultures and spiritual values. On a more positive note, it has also led to European-American support of some of the Native American causes during the civil rights era, and it may have paved the way for the establishment of the restitution policy, which has given Native people the opportunity to push their claims for land that had been previously taken from them by the government.

SEE ALSO:

Colonialism; Dutch Colonists; England; France; Indian Policy, U.S.; Noble Savage; Removal Policy; Termination Policy; Spain; "Vanishing Americans."

EUROPEAN ATTITUDES TOWARD INDIGENOUS PEOPLES

The attitudes held by western Europe's imperial powers toward American Indians differed little from their attitudes about indigenous people in other parts of the world, such as Africa and Asia. The Portuguese, Spanish, French, Dutch, English, and Russians assumed that Christianity made them superior to pagans (people who are not Christians).

The "age of exploration," when Europeans first entered the North American continent, occurred during periods of spiritual reawakening and religious reform in Europe. The attitudes of the Inquisition, which abhorred anything and anyone not Catholic and brought about the expulsion of Mus-

European stereotypes of Indians are frequently perpetuated for commercial purposes. This sign adorns a tattoo parlor in Puerto Rico.

lims and Jews from Spain, reverberated throughout Europe and the Americas. Thus bolstered by their religious prejudices, European immigrants assumed Indians to be inferior and demonized Native people as savages and agents of Satan. Europeans believed that this status justified the captivity and enslavement of Native people, even though certain members of the clergy, notably Francisco de Vitoria and Bartolomé de Las Casas, debated the issue of slavery in church doctrine. The stereotype of the wild uncivilized Indian depicted in various early European and colonial writings continues in modern media.

European and colonial writers also created and supported the image of the "noble savage"—Indian men exhibiting a stoical and proud bearing, Indian women as shy but fierce maidens, work drudges, and wise healers. Historians tended to dismiss the idea that Indians could be patriots whose anger and nobility were fueled by their respect for their own land and by the disrespect shown by the new land-grasping immigrants.

In his journals, Columbus describes the *indios* as gentle, willing to share, and virtually without weapons; he then calls for enslaving and converting them. This pattern was repeated by the other European powers. To Europeans, the Western Hemisphere was the long-imagined El Dorado, a place of fabulous potential wealth. Europeans believed that conquering the forests and "savages" was justified and supported by Christianity, which also was taken to support seizing land from the Indi-

ans for settlements and expanding commerce.

Indian spirituality, realized daily in storytelling and through a value system involving the natural and supernatural worlds, was condemned as going against the teachings of the church. In North America, towns of "praying Indians" became a refuge for those who accepted Christianity as their only choice over annihilation. Yet, nowhere in the Americas did conversion guarantee immunity from hostile Europeans.

entado, compuesto y dirigido por Diego Rivera, trabajaron en equipo sus camaradas pintores.

This mural by Diego Rivera dramatizes the oppression of the indigenous peoples of Mexico by their Spanish conquerors. Much of Rivera's art illustrates the relationship between the conqueror and the conquered.

Europeans also perceived the Indian culture through their own ideas regarding landownership and use. Whether hunter-gatherers or stable farmers, the Indians understood the earth as a maternal being. Colonists never comprehended how a sale of land was inconceivable to Indians; to the Indians, land could not be sold since one person or even a group of people could not "own" the earth. When such transactions occurred, the Indian community believed it had, instead, entered into a land use agreement. As colonists frequently and illegally invaded the land of the Indians' ancestors, hostilities erupted.

Cultures also clashed because Indian culture did not value the Europeans' notion of work for personal and community industry and spiritual benefit. Settlers, perceiving hunting and fishing as recreation, called Indian men lazy as their wives labored in the fields. Since the Europeans saw the Indians as not "using" the land, they felt justified in simply taking it.

But not all colonists saw and treated the Indians the same way: Cruelty took different forms under Spanish and English dominion. English settlers outnumbered Iberian conquistador-adventurers and French, and later Russian, traders and clerics. As the conquering Spanish bred with the Natives through generations, socioeconomic divisions were made between those of purebred Spanish descent, Indian descent, and mixed descent. The *mestizos*, products of this continental mixing, were despised by the Spanish upper class in both Americas. Worse off were those of full Indian descent; no matter what they did economically, they were viewed and often scorned as a cultural lower class.

French traders, unlike the English, readily married Indian women. Many of these mixed families were regarded as relatives by the Indians. French clerics helped enforce male dominance in all aspects of family and marital relations, deeming women's powers in land and political decision making improper and un-Christian. This went against many Native customs; in a number of tribes, women held the land and were a major force in politics.

As later Indian removal policies pushed Indians further and further away from Euro-American settlements, a sense of romance for the image of the "vanishing Red man" grew. The Indian warrior was memorialized on coins and "cigar store"

figurines, and Indian women were often depicted as bereaved or betrayed maidens preparing to commit suicide by throwing themselves into a ravine or over a waterfall. But the Indian Removal Act of 1830 confirmed that the United States had no place for its original inhabitants. As westward expansion continued, so did the demand that Indians accept reservation life.

The language of genocide has long been used by European-Americans to define Indian life and has thus determined Native people's survival strategies. "Killing savages" was General Jeffrey Amherst's intention in 1763 by providing the Seneca with smallpox-exposed blankets. A century later, the phrase "the only good Indian is a dead Indian" became a popular remark. And William H. Pratt, founder of the Carlisle Indian School in 1879, proclaimed, "Kill the Indian and save the man." That is, wipe out all of an individual Indian's heritage and make him or her into a Euro-American as much as possible.

In trying to follow this last policy, the boarding school movement attempted to assimilate Indians into American society by means that were degrading. Pupils were often kidnapped from families, and their education prepared them only for agricultural work, not for the jobs created by the Industrial Revolution. Alcohol abuse, too, had ravaged Indian communities for almost as long as European diseases, with whites blaming Indians for its results, overlooking their lack of physiological resistance to alcohol and alien bacteria.

In modern times, non-Native groups practicing Indian culture attract adherents. Euro-American groups are particularly proud of the authenticity of their attempts to "honor" Native Americans. Somewhat outside of the mainstream culture, Indian spiritual and medicine traditions have been adopted into New Age philosophies, a fact unpopular among Indians who have seen their cultures misappropriated for costume parties and commercialized sweat lodge "ceremonies." Indians are distressed and angered that whites presume the sacredness of their ways can be playfully distorted and so easily discarded.

Public sympathy for American Indian sovereignty and cultural issues increased after the Wounded Knee siege of 1973 on the Pine Ridge Reservation in South Dakota. Some Hollywood movies like

Members of the American Indian Movement (AIM) protest outside the Metrodome in Minneapolis on January 26, 1992, at the Superbowl, objecting to the use of an Indian as the mascot of the Washington Redskins professional football team. Long-held negative attitudes and romanticized ideas about Native peoples and cultures have popularized Indians as savage warriors or as members of a "vanishing" breed of Americans.

Dances with Wolves (1990) and *Thunderheart* (1992), independent productions like *Pow Wow Highway* (1988), and television documentaries like *500 Nations* have also rectified some past media damage with their positive and more realistic portrayal of Indian life.

Nevertheless, non-Indians remain devoted to their "right of free enterprise" when faced with Indians contesting treaty rights that affect recreational fishing and mining natural resources. Indians are treated with contempt when they are thought to stand in the way of "progress," as in the case of East Coast Indians who rose to protect community shorelines from realtors. Non-Indians have reacted jealously to the success of reservation gambling casinos and to affirmative action programs, especially when Indians want to hire mostly Indians for construction jobs on reservations where unemployment is high. Pot hunting and other sorts of vandalizing of Indian burial sites produce income for

many non-Indians who have no respect for the dead. Furthermore, many whites still persist in acknowledging an Indian only as someone dressed in buckskin and feathers, not as a teamster, physician, rock musician, or teacher.

In the contemporary United States, non-Native children enjoy the Disney animated feature *Pocahontas* (1995), hum its tunes, and cheer for the Indians instead of the white men. The movie's popularity—with its subtly racist romanticizing of the Indians and transformation of Pocahontas into a tanned-looking princess with European features—may suggest that non-Indian attitudes toward Native Americans still have a long way to go.

— R. Welburn

SEE ALSO:

Alcoholism; Boarding Schools; Ceremonies, Exploitation of; Cigar-Store Indian; Colonialism; New Age Movement; Removal Act, Indian; "Vanishing Americans."

SUGGESTED READINGS:

Anderson, Karen. *Chain Her by One Foot: The Subjugation of Women in Seventeenth-Century New France.* London: Routledge, 1991.

Berkhofer, Robert F., Jr. *The White Man's Indian: Images of the American Indian from Columbus to the Present.* New York: Knopf, 1978.

Churchill, Ward. *Fantasies of the Master Race: Literature, Cinema and the Colonization of American Indians.* M. Annette Jaimes, ed. Monroe, ME: Common Courage Press, 1992.

Deloria, Vine, Jr. *God Is Red: A Native View of Religion.* Golden, CO: Fulcrum Books, 1994.

Echo-Hawk, Roger C., and Walter R. Echo-Hawk. *Battlefields and Burial Grounds: The Indian Struggle to Protect Ancestral Graves in the United States.* New York: Lerner, 1994.

FADDEN, JOHN KAHIONHES (1938–)

John Kahionhes Fadden, a Mohawk; his father, Ray Fadden; and their families have played a major role in preserving and reviving Mohawk language and culture through artistic and educational endeavors spanning much of the last half of the twentieth century. Their efforts have reached people across the United States and in many other countries through correspondence and books, while the Faddens' major impact in upstate New York has been through the family's Six Nations Indian Museum at Onchiota.

Born in Massena, New York, John Kahionhes Fadden earned a bachelor's degree in fine art at the Rochester Institute of Technology (1961) and did graduate work at St. Lawrence University and the State University of New York at Plattsburgh. As his artistic talents developed, Fadden melded with them an intense political awareness of the changes taking place in Akwesasne, his homeland, where he often illustrated for the newspaper *Akwesasne Notes.* His art also portrays worldwide indigenous and ecological themes.

John Fadden's artwork had reached audiences around the world in fifty-two books (including eighteen book covers) by the early 1990s, thirty exhibitions, eleven calendars, and other media.

Ray and John Fadden, Mohawks. The Fadden family founded the Six Nations Indian Museum at Onchiota, New York.

Fadden also has been a leader in efforts to provide Iroquois-produced materials for schools in New York State. Until early 1994, he taught middle-school art for thirty-two years in the Saranac Central School system.

John Fadden's wife, Eva, is an accomplished carver in wood and soapstone. His son David is a graphic artist who, by his early twenties, had illustrated several books and magazines.

SEE ALSO:

Akwesasne Notes; Fadden, Ray Tehanetorens; Iroquois Confederacy; Mohawk.

FADDEN, RAY TEHANETORENS
(1910–)

Ray Tehanetorens Fadden has been a principal figure during most of the last half of the twentieth century in the preservation of Mohawk and other Iroquois language and culture.

As founders of the Six Nations Indian Museum at Onchiota, New York, the Fadden family has been active since the 1950s in cultural affairs in New York State. Fadden's dedication to teaching began in the 1940s with the founding of the Akwesasne Mohawk Counselor Organization, which taught Mohawk language and culture to several generations. Fadden has prepared twenty-six pamphlets and forty-two charts detailing Iroquois history as part of the Six Nations Museum Series.

Much of Ray Fadden's life and that of his wife and family have been dedicated to fighting degradation of the environment in the Adirondack Mountains, their home. Fadden says that acid rain and other pollutants are destroying the abundance and variety of life in the forest. "If you kill the forest life, you kill your own grandchildren."

To many of his former students, Ray Fadden is a living legend. "He was father, grandfather, teacher [and] friend to three generations of Mohawks," said Ron LaFrance, a Mohawk and a former student of Fadden.

SEE ALSO:

Fadden, John Kahionhes; Iroquois Confederacy; Mohawk.

FALLEN TIMBERS, BATTLE OF

Following the close of the American Revolution in 1783, the new U.S. government turned to dealing with its conflicts with Native American tribes southwest and northwest of the new nation. The tribes in the Southwest, especially the powerful Creek tribe, were bargained with in treaties. This policy of making treaties was President George Washington's idea. He favored strengthening ties with friendly tribes but hammering resisting tribes. Thomas Jefferson argued for an even harsher policy for dealing with Indians. He thought that all tribes must first experience a "thorough drubbing"; and then, after experiencing the power of the United States, their continued peacefulness could be maintained through "liberal and repeated presents."

In the area northwest of the new nation, in Ohio and in Kentucky, the Miami and Wabash tribes violently opposed expansion into their territory. Between 1783 and 1790, fifteen hundred white men, women, and children were killed or taken into captivity. In addition, two thousand horses were stolen and fifty thousand dollars of damage was done to property.

In 1790, the U.S. government sent its first military force against the Miami and Wabash tribes. A force made up of three hundred federal troops and more than one thousand untrained militia under Brevet Brigadier General Josiah Harmar moved on the Miami towns. They were met by an Indian force under the Miami leader, Little Turtle, who was called Michikinikwa in his language. Harmar suffered a defeat in which 150 soldiers were killed and many more were wounded.

In 1791, a second force was sent against the Indians under the command of Major General Arthur St. Claire. General St. Claire had a force of fourteen hundred men, many of whom were again untrained militia. Before sending St. Claire off, President Washington gave him a warning based on his own experience from the French and Indian War. "Beware of surprise," he cautioned St. Claire. St. Claire advanced on the Miami towns slowly and took up a strong defensive position with cannon in the center of his line. On the morning of November 4, 1791, Little Turtle led a strong Indian force against St. Claire's position. St. Claire and his men fired from ranks, while Little Turtle's men fired from behind trees. After three hours of fierce fighting, it became clear to St. Claire that if he stayed in position, his entire force would be wiped out. He started a withdrawal that eventually turned into a rout. When the battle was over, the U.S. Army had suffered its worst defeat. Out of the force of 1,400 men, 637 were killed and 263 were wounded. St. Claire also lost his cannons and all of his supplies.

After this defeat, many senators and representatives in Congress argued for a treaty with the Indians that would allow Native peoples to keep their land. But President Washington still favored the plan of gaining a military victory over the Indians so the new nation could expand west. He authorized a third expedition against the Miami and Wabash tribes under the command of General "Mad Anthony" Wayne. Wayne was a hero from the Revolutionary War who had gained fame when he captured the strong British fort at Stony Point in July of 1779. Wayne realized that if he was to be successful, he would need troops who were well trained. During 1792 and 1793, he trained his army of three thousand men and built up his supplies.

In July of 1793, the U.S. government tried one last time to gain a peace treaty with the Indians at the Sandusky Conference. Little was accomplished, however, because the Indian chiefs were resolute that the Ohio River must be the boundary beyond which the whites could not cross, as was the understanding of the Fort Stanwix Agreement of 1768.

Set on war, Wayne moved his force west and built a fort near the Miami towns on a branch of the Maumee River. He named the position Fort Greenville after his Revolutionary War friend, Nathaniel Green. He also established other forts as he slowly advanced into Miami territory.

On June 29, 1794, Little Turtle and a body of Miami warriors attacked Fort Recovery. The Indians were beaten back and suffered heavy casualties. Because of this defeat, Little Turtle was replaced as war leader by another Miami leader, Turkey Foot.

Wayne continued to prepare for battle with the Indians. He also met with British forces in the area to make sure that they would remain out of the fighting. In mid-August of 1794, Wayne's army finally entered into battle with the main Indian force at a site called Fallen Timbers. The site was so named because a tornado had created a great

tangle of fallen trees near the rapids of the Maumee River. It was in this tangle that the Indians took up their position. Instead of attacking, Wayne waited for three days. Many of the Indians had to leave their position to seek food. Those Indians who remained were weak with hunger. Finally, on August 20, 1794, Wayne and his force attacked. A fierce bayonet charge forced the Indians out of the trees and onto the open prairie, where they were easy prey for Wayne's mounted volunteers. Turkey Foot was killed, and the Indians fled to the British fort nearby. Before the battle, the British commander had assured the Indians that they could seek refuge in the fort if the battle went badly. But the commander failed to honor his promise, and the Indians were slaughtered right outside the walls of the fort.

Out of his force of three thousand men, Wayne lost thirty-eight dead and about one hundred wounded. Although there was no exact count, it is known that hundreds of Indians died in the battle, and the power of the Miami and Wabash tribes was lost. Wayne burned the Miami towns and destroyed five thousand acres (two thousand hectares) of crops. On August 3, 1795, the Miami and Wabash chiefs ceded all of Ohio and most of Indiana to the United States.

— T. Colonnese

SEE ALSO:

French and Indian War; Indiana; Kentucky; Little Turtle; Miami; Ohio.

FAMILY, ROLE IN NATIVE SOCIETY

Families are very important in all Native American cultures and often function as economic units and as the building blocks of government and society. They are joined across village and band boundaries by systems of clan relations, which serve to tie together confederate political systems. It would be virtually impossible to give detailed discussions of families as they function in the hundreds of Native cultures in North America. By looking at three representative groups, however—the Iroquois, the Wyandots (Hurons), and the Apaches—it is

This mother and child live on Baffin Island in the far north. Today, Native mothers do not have to live in fear that their children will be taken from them and sent far away to government boarding schools where their children would be raised outside of their Native culture.

A father and child in the far north. In some traditional Native cultures, uncles assume primary responsibility for a child, leaving a father and his children to form a close emotional bond free of many kinds of pressures that are common in other cultures.

possible to get a picture of the extent to which families shape Native societies.

The Iroquois

The Iroquois Confederacy is basically a kinship state. The Iroquois are bound together by a clan and chieftain system that is supported by a similar linguistic base. Through the "hearth" that consisted of a mother and her children, women played a profound role in Iroquois political life. Each hearth was part of a wider group called an *otiianer*, and two or more otiianers constituted a clan. The word *otiianer* refers to the female heirs to the chieftain titles of the League, the fifty authorized names for the chiefs of the Iroquois, passed through the female side of the otiianer. The otiianer women selected one of the males within their group to fill a vacated seat in the League.

Such a matrilineal system was headed by a "clan mother." All the sons and daughters of a particular clan were related through uterine families (where the children of a family have the same mother but different fathers) that lived far apart. In this system, a husband went to live with his wife's family, and their children became members of the mother's clan by right of birth. The oldest daughter of the head of a clan sometimes succeeded her mother at her death upon the judgment of the clan. Through matrilineal descent, the Iroquois formed cohesive political groups that had little to do with where people lived or from what village the hearths originated.

All authority sprang from the people of the various clans that made up a nation. The women who headed these clans appointed the male delegates and deputies who spoke for the clans at tribal meetings. After consultation within the clan, issues and questions were formulated and subsequently debated in council.

A Florida Seminole elder and child. In many traditional Native cultures, the entire community participates in child rearing.

Iroquois political philosophy is rooted in the concept that all life is unified spiritually with the natural environment and other forces surrounding people. The Iroquois believe that the spiritual power of one person is limited, but when combined with other individuals in a hearth, otiianer, or clan, spiritual power is enhanced.

Whenever a person died either by natural causes or force, through murder or war, the "public" power was diminished. To maintain the strength of the group, families often replaced the dead by adopting captives of war. This practice of keeping clans at full strength through natural increase or adoption ensured the power and durability of the matrilineal system as well as the kinship state.

This Apache girl's puberty ceremony, at White River, Arizona, is a community effort and is proudly and vigorously advertised by the tribe.

Child rearing was an important way to instill political philosophy in the youth of the Iroquois. The ideal Iroquois personality was a person who had loyalty to the group but was independent and autonomous. Iroquois people were trained to enter a society that was egalitarian, with power more equally distributed between male and female, young and old, than in Euro-American society. European society emphasized dominance and command structures, while Iroquois society was interested in collaborative behavior.

The Hurons (Wyandots)

As with the Iroquois, the Huron (Wyandot) clans—Porcupine, Snake, Deer, Beaver, Hawk, Turtle, Bear, and Wolf—created relationships through family ties across the boundaries of the four confederated Huron nations. Members of each clan could trace their ancestry to a common origin through the female line. In each village, clan members elected a civil chief and a war chief. The titles were carried through the female family line but bestowed on men, again resembling the Iroquois. While the titles were hereditary in that sense, they did not

pass from head to head of a particular family, as in most European monarchies. When time came to choose a leader, members of each clan segment in a particular village had a choice of several candidates, among whom, according to author Bruce Trigger, personal qualities counted most heavily, for example, "intelligence, oratorical ability, reputation for generosity and, above all, performance as a warrior."

If a village included more than one clan segment (most did, but not all), the elected leaders of each segment formed a village council. The council resolved issues through debate leading to consensus on purely local issues. Each of the four tribes, including several villages, held councils that included all the village civil and war chiefs.

The four nations—the Attignawantan, Arendarhonon, Attigneenongahac, and Tahontaeanrat—also held a central council, which, according to historian Bruce Trigger, probably consisted of all the village chiefs representing all the clans. Compared to the Iroquois Grand Council, we know very little about how the Huron Grand Council operated. It is likely that the Huron Confederacy was looser than the Iroquois since the central council met only once a year, usually for several weeks in the spring, although emergency meetings could be called at any time. The meeting of the central council was meant to bind the four nations and served as much as a social occasion for families as a legislative session. Its proceedings were embellished with feasts to install new village headmen, meetings between old friends, singing, dancing, and war feasts. The central council dealt with issues that affected all four nations in common, such as treaty negotiations and trade with Europeans.

The Apaches

Apache society was centered on groups of two to six extended families based around the mothers' families, a unit sometimes called a *gota*. Members of the gota lived together, and members of the different households cooperated in hunting and farming. A gota was usually led by a headman who assumed his status over several years by general agreement of the extended families in the gota. The headman in some cases inherited the title of "true chief." He would not retain the position, however, unless he displayed leadership. If no qualified headman was raised through inheritance, a consensus would form in favor of another leader who would be informally "elected" by members of the gota. Headmen were invariably male, but women exercised influence as political advisers, and it was their society and kinship lineages that maintained the Apaches' matrilineal society.

A headman could wield considerable influence, but only if the people in the extended families he led were willing to follow his advice, which could include detailed lectures on how to hunt, the techniques of agriculture, and who should work with whom. He also coordinated labor for hunting and foraging, advised parties engaged in disputes, and was sought out for advice regarding who should marry whom. At times, the wife of a chief would become, in effect, a subchief. As a chief aged, he was not only charged with maintaining exemplary behavior, but with identifying young men who might become leaders in the future. He was expected to tutor younger men in the responsibilities of leadership. A chief was also charged with aiding the poor, oftentimes by coordinating distribution of donations from more affluent members of the

gota. If two or more gotas engaged in conflict, their headmen were charged with resolving the dispute.

Each Apache was a member not only of a gota, but also one of sixty-two matrilineal clans that overlapped the individual settlements. Members of one's clan (and, in some cases, others identified as being close to it) helped each other in survival tasks and usually did not intermarry. Such a system resembles that of many peoples in the eastern woodlands, such as the Cherokees, Hurons, and Iroquois.

— B. E. Johansen

SEE ALSO:
Apache; Cherokee; Iroquois Confederacy; Wyandot.

SUGGESTED READINGS:
Colden, Cadwallader. *The History of the Five Nations of Canada* [1765]. New York: Amsterdam Book Co., 1902.
Corkran, David H. *The Cherokee Frontier: Conflict and Survival, 1740-62.* Norman: University of Oklahoma Press, 1962.
Fenton, William N., et. al., eds. *Symposium on Cherokee and Iroquois Culture.* Smithsonian Institution Bureau of Ethnology Bulletin 180. Washington, D.C.: Government Printing Office, 1961.
McKee, Jesse O., and Jon A. Schlenker. *The Choctaws: Cultural Evolution of a Native American Tribe.* Jackson: University Press of Mississippi, 1980.
Trigger, Bruce G. *The Children of Aataentsic: A History of the Huron People.* Montreal: McGill-Queen's University Press, 1976.
Wallace, Anthony F. C. *The Death and Rebirth of the Seneca.* New York: Vintage, 1972.

FANCY DANCE AND FANCY SHAWL DANCE

The men's Fancy Dance and the women's Fancy Shawl Dance are the most exuberant styles of all the popular dances that are featured in the Native American powwow circuits. The Fancy Dance is very appropriately named because the detailed footwork and ornate costumes, along with the high-stepping spins and acrobatic body moves, are everything that the word *fancy* implies; it is a

A Sioux Fancy Dancer, displaying powwow regalia that can cost thousands of dollars and be worn in dance competitions for prize money at intertribal competition powwows throughout the North American continent.

Women displaying regalia for the Women's Fancy Shawl Dance at a powwow at Casa Grande, Arizona.

dance, and it is very fancy indeed. Fancy dancers must be in top physical shape to perform the intricate, fast, and acrobatic motions required of the Fancy Dance. They must move their feet and bodies in time to the drums, balancing their footwork from the left to the right in beats of four.

The Fancy Dance developed from traditional war dances such as the Omaha Dance, Crow Dance, and Straight Dance, all of which were performed among the Osage, Pawnee, Omaha, and Ponca Indians of the Oklahoma prairie during the late nineteenth and early twentieth centuries. These war dances were practiced among organizations of established warriors whose ceremonies enacted courageous war deeds. The western Oklahoma tribes began developing increasingly elaborate versions of these ceremonial war dances, and the exclusive rights of these ceremonies, as performed only by men, eventually expanded to include women as well.

The earliest forms of the Fancy Dance were not just known as a particular type of choreography (that of intricate footwork) but were also known by the types of costumes and accessories. The early costumes for the male Fancy Dance included color-coordinated bustles (material gathered in a kind of bow or array) at the waist and shoulders, along with small bustles on the upper arms. During the 1930s and 1940s, bustles were much smaller than ones seen today, and they were often made out of pheasant feathers. Many fancy dancers from the 1930s to the 1950s wore a feather crest headdress (an upright double row of feathers worn on the head), while other fancy dancers wore a deer hair roach (a row or strip of hair) attached to a headband. The deer hair roach had completely replaced the feather crest headdress by the 1960s and was redesigned to include the "bobber," a device that bounces in response to movement, thus giving the dancer greater freedom of movement as well. The feather bustles, attached to the arms, back, and shoulders, had undergone a significant change as well, using larger feathers, such as turkey or eagle. Sometime during the 1970s, these feathers were dyed in an assortment of colors, which added new and exciting elements to the costumes.

Women's Fancy Shawl costumes always include the wearing of a shawl, which is usually of a bright color and draped with fringes. Unlike the male fancy dancers, the female Fancy Shawl dancers do not wear the ornate and dazzling feather bustles. Nor do they wear the deer hair roach headdresses. Instead, female Fancy Shawl dancers can usually be seen wearing a single feather, a pair of feathers, or any number of various other types of hair ornamentation, such as beaded braid wraps or barrettes. Fancy Shawl dancers wear cloth dresses, sometimes with belts, capes, leggings, or moccasins.

SEE ALSO:
Dance, American Indian; Feathers and Featherwork.

FEATHERS AND FEATHERWORK

The Native peoples of the Americas are known for their featherwork. The transformation of feathers into cultural objects is a significant act, one that contributes to the unique identity and lifestyle of a group. It is difficult, however, to classify the uses of feathers and the different types of featherwork among Native American peoples. As with so many other aspects of Native American life, featherwork is individual to each nation, even to each person. Various tribes have developed distinctive styles when working with feathers, and the articles they make are used differently.

Nevertheless, it is possible to describe some common practices among tribes. Featherwork may be used for personal adornment, for significant social rituals, in religious practices, and as an expression of group identity. Often, a group will invest feathers with symbolism and meaning specific to that group. One common belief is that a feather has the characteristics of the bird it came from.

A Hopi prayer feather, displayed on a mano, a corn grinding stone.

This young Eagle Dancer is a member of a Head Start class at Laguna Pueblo, New Mexico.

Here featherwork is seen combined with the use of mirrors at a powwow on the Siletz Reservation in Oregon.

them into cloaks and headgear. The early Southeastern tribes, including the Cherokees, used feathers in many different ways. These tribes believed that owls, hummingbirds, turkeys, and buzzards all have unique attributes that are symbolized by their feathers and that the feathers are powerful spiritual instruments.

Traditionally, healers have used feathers in their ceremonies; contemporary healers may wear particular kinds of feathers in their hatbands to signal their specialties. A buzzard feather, for example, might indicate the ability to cure bullet wounds. Feathers are also used ceremonially; for instance, the Cherokee Eagle Dance uses an eagle feather wand to symbolize peace.

For some Native peoples, the symbolism of the feather remains intertwined with all aspects of life. The Hopis, for example, associate feathers with clouds and rain. Feathers adorn costumes, offerings, prayer sticks, and kachina dolls that represent spirits of the Hopis' ancestors. Feathers are also found in decorations on basketry and pottery.

Feathers have been used to signify war honors as well. In Ponca tradition, the placement and angle of an eagle feather or feathers worn on the head has different significance. Feathers worn upright on the crown indicate the number of captures made, while feathers worn low on the head and inclined to the left denote a leader.

Today, the use of feathers is largely ceremonial. In the Native American Church, for example, participants use peyote fans constructed with feathers and beaded handles. Intertribal powwows feature dancers with feathers in their costumes. Both men

The Native peoples of South America and Hawaii are known for their spectacular featherwork. Hawaiian royalty wore feather cloaks and helmets and carried *kahilis,* or feathered scepters. Amazonian tribes use feathers creatively in a variety of ways. In one group, people cover their bodies with eagle down; another group is known for its unusual, eye-catching feather headdresses.

Among the Native peoples of North America, featherwork has also been a widespread form of expression. In the sixteenth and seventeenth centuries, southern tribes wove turkey, duck, and swan feathers into a fiber backing and then fashioned and women carry feather fans, and the "fancy dancers" wear costumes made with elaborate feather bustles.

In the past, feathers were obtained in different ways. Birds were hunted and trapped, but they also were domesticated and raised to ensure a supply of feathers for various purposes. Today, the use of feathers for traditional purposes has come into conflict with laws designed to protect endangered bird species. This controversy came to a head in 1974, when some powwow attendees were arrested by agents of the U.S. Fish and Wildlife Service for selling eagle feathers. They were found guilty and fined, and their feathers were confiscated. This created a shock wave in Native American communities, and many dance costumes and other sacred or ceremonial objects were put away for fear that their possession would be considered illegal.

The resulting criticism of this action led to the American Indian Religious Freedom Act (PL 95-341), which was passed by Congress in 1978. It ensures the rights of Native Americans to practice their ceremonial and traditional rites and to possess and use sacred objects. However, since it is still illegal to sell some feathers and hunt some birds without a permit, it can be difficult to obtain or create ceremonial objects.

— M. A. Stout

SEE ALSO:
Dance, American Indian; Fancy Dance and Fancy Shawl Dance; Kachina; Regalia; Native American Church.

FEDERAL LAND

Land for which the U.S. government maintains responsibility is considered "federal land." This land includes military bases, federal prisons and other institutions, and national parks and national preservation areas, among others.

These lands were acquired from Indian nations through a variety of means, such as treaties. In some cases, the government simply evicted Indian groups whose people had been living on the land for centuries. Sometimes, the government designated an individual member of the tribe a "chief" and tricked that person into signing away land that he had been led to believe would be shared rather than ceded completely.

In some of the treaties in which land was ceded to the United States, it was stipulated that when the United States no longer had use for the land, it would revert to the Indian nations. One such treaty was the Fort Laramie Treaty of 1868, in which the Sioux people were granted rights to federal lands. When the United States refused to abide by the terms of the treaty, the Sioux pressed their case against the government. The United States has been ordered to pay the Sioux for the land that the government took, but the Sioux have refused to accept money for land—the Black Hills of South Dakota—that they consider to be sacred.

Governmental agencies are responsible for the upkeep and care of federal land. Many of the federal lands are maintained by the Bureau of Land Management. Other agencies caring for federal land include the U.S. Forestry Service, the U.S. Department of Fish and Wildlife, and the National Park Service. Other land is under the care of the U.S. Armed Forces and is used for military bases, while some land, such as that used for federal prisons, is under the jurisdiction of the U.S. Justice Department.

When military bases are closed because of federal funding cuts, the land is sometimes auctioned to the highest bidder, and the federal government receives the money, as was the case of the sale of Fort Chaffee in Arkansas. In recent years, American Indians have claimed that they have been discriminated against in the bidding for such lands.

Alcatraz Island, in San Francisco Bay, is a prime example of federal land that many believe the government should have been made available to Indian people. Alcatraz was the site of a federal prison until it was closed and the land was vacated. In the late 1960s and early 1970s, Indians occupied the land. They claimed Alcatraz Island by right of treaty as abandoned federal property, according to a provision in the Fort Laramie Treaty of 1868. The occupation gained media attention for Indian issues but was ultimately unsuccessful.

Other disputes have arisen between Indians and the federal government over issues involving land use and over questions of whether or not a particular tract of land is Indian land or federal land. In

Military posts make up a small portion of federal land once inhabited by Native people but taken over by the government. Here, Indians from Wyoming visit the old fort at Governor's Island in New York in 1924, upon their return from a trip to England.

Nevada, for example, the federal government has refused to abide by the provisions of the Treaty of Ruby Valley with the Western Shoshone Nation. The government has placed certain lands belonging to the Western Shoshones under the jurisdiction of the Bureau of Land Management, which has caused a conflict between non-Indian cattle ranchers and the Western Shoshone Nation. The United States treats the land as government land and leases it to ranchers in the area. For twenty years, Carrie and Mary Dann, members of the Western Shoshones, have refused to pay government fees in order to graze their cattle on what they consider their own land. In return, the U.S. government has repeatedly harassed them by confiscating their cattle. These incidents have gained media attention, especially in the American Indian press, and the Dann sisters have become articulate advocates for Indian rights.

Another land issue involves ownership of the Black Hills, a sacred site for the Sioux. The site has a national monument, Mount Rushmore, which features the heads of four U.S. presidents carved into the side of a mountain. Mount Rushmore has become a major tourist attraction, but the Sioux consider the monument a desecration of their sacred hills. The Sioux proved in the U.S. Court of Claims that the Black Hills had been taken from them illegally by the United States, and they have been awarded a monetary judgment as compensation. The Sioux , however, have refused to accept the money and are demanding to have their land returned.

Other issues regarding the use of federal land continue to create controversy. The appropriateness of using the site of a massacre of Indians as a tourist attraction has been one such issue. In 1995, a bill was introduced into Congress that would create the Wounded Knee Memorial Park in South Dakota, at the site of the 1890 massacre of more than three hundred Indian children, women, and elders by the U.S. Army. Advocates for Indian rights are working to defeat the bill.

— S. S. Davis

FEDERALLY RECOGNIZED NATIONS AND TRIBES

Federal recognition is a status acknowledged for Indian nations that have been recognized by the United States government as legitimate governing bodies of particular Indian people. Federal recognition also means that the U.S. government maintains government-to-government relationships with the recognized Indian nations, as it would with any other separate nation, such as Britain, France, or Japan. Recognition preserves certain rights that have been guaranteed to an Indian nation by treaties, executive orders, or special acts of Congress or that have been determined by the courts to be available to the tribe and its members.

Indian nations were proclaimed to be "domestic dependent nations" in the U.S. Supreme Court case *Cherokee Nation v. Georgia,* 1831. Ironically, however, only a generation or two earlier, it was the Indian nations that had helped the United States to be recognized as a legitimate nation by the other nations of the world. This is because the Indian nations were already recognized as legitimate governing nations by the international community. By entering into treaties of peace and friendship with Indian nations, the fledgling U.S. government gained legitimacy.

Over the years, other treaties were signed between the United States and Indian nations for various purposes. These included allowing for the construction of roads through Indian lands, for trade and commerce, and for land acquisition. Federal recognition of an Indian nation is often based on these treaties.

Other Indian nations have gained federal recognition through an executive order, by a presidential proclamation, or by legislation that mentions

Lemuel Occum Fielding, a traditional leader of the Mohicans, meets with Cato Sells, Commissioner of Indian Affairs in Washington, D.C., in 1924, to present a claim for 16 acres (6.4 hectares) of the business district of Norwich, Connecticut. The land, then valued at approximately two million dollars, had been deeded to the Mohicans in 1830.

the tribe. Some nations, such as the Mashpees, are not recognized by the federal government but are recognized by their state governments. Some nations lost federal recognition during the termination era of the 1950s, when the United States sought to end its government-to-government relationship with some Indian nations by one-sided Congressional action. Some of these "terminated" Indian nations have not regained federal recognition. Other tribes have never entered into treaties with the United States and therefore have never been acknowledged.

The Federal Acknowledgment Project of 1978 allows for a formal procedure through which Indian nations, bands, and communities may seek federal recognition. Hundreds of such Indian groups are awaiting the results of legislative action or lawsuits to obtain federal recognition. (One such tribe, the Lumbees, recently received federal recogniation.) All nations filing for federal recognition must abide by U.S. procedures for recognition purposes. Some nations have petitioned for recognition but have not yet obtained it.

Federally recognized nations may obtain funding from the United States for certain programs. Some of these programs are for housing, food, economic development, and health care. Members of federally recognized nations are also allowed to use the Indian Health Services facilities.

In addition, federally recognized nations have legal jurisdiction over their lands. Some of the lands are on Indian reservations, while others are lands the United States government holds in trust for the particular nations. Crimes committed on federally recognized Indian land may be tried in the tribes' own court system or in federal court. As upheld in recent Supreme Court decisions, the states have no criminal jurisdiction on federally recognized Indian land unless a compact has been entered into between the state and the Indian nation. Many Indian nations have entered into such compacts for the benefit of public safety, with both Indian and state law enforcement officers being cross-deputized. This allows them to uphold public order within lands shared by both an Indian nation and a state.

The federal government issues cards, called Certificates of Degree of Indian Blood (CDIB), to members of federally recognized Indian nations.

Federally recognized nations, listed by state, are as follows:

Alabama: Poarch Band of Creek.

Alaska: Ahtna, Incorporated; Aleut Corporation; Annette Island Reserve; Arctic Slope Regional Corporation; Bering Straits Native Corporation; Bristol Bay Native Corporation; Calista Corporation; Chugach Natives, Inc.; Cook Inlet Region, Inc.; Doyon, Limited; Koniag, Inc.; NANA Regional Corporation; Sealaska Regional Corporation; Thirteenth Regional Corporation. Many tribal communities, towns, and villages in Alaska also have federal recognition.

Arizona: San Carlos Apache Tribe of the San Carlos Reservation; Tonto Apache Tribe of Arizona; White Mountain Apache Tribe of the Fort Apache Reservation; Cocopah Tribe of Arizona; Havasupai Tribe of the Havasupai Reservation; Hopi Tribe of Arizona; Hualapai Tribe of the Hualapai Indian Reservation; Colorado River Indian Tribes of the Colorado River Indian Reservation, Arizona and California (Mojave and Chemehuevi); Fort McDowell Mojave-Apache Indian Community of Fort McDowell Indian Reservations (Mojave, Apache, and Yavapai).

Also, Navajo Tribe of Arizona, New Mexico, and Utah; Kaibab Band of Pauite Indians of the Kaibab Indian Reservation; Gila River Pima–Maricopa Indian Community of the Gila River Reservation of Arizona; Salt River Pima–Maricopa Indian Community of the Salt River Reservation; Quechan Tribe of the Fort Yuma Indian Reservation; Ak Chin Indian Community of Papago Indians of the Maricopa, Ak Chin Reservation; Tohono O'odham Nation of Arizona; Pascua Yaqui Tribe of Arizona; Yavapai–Apache Indian Community of the Camp Verde Reservation; Yavapai-Prescott Tribe of the Yavapai Reservation.

California: Agua Caliente Band of Cahuilla Indians of the Agua Caliente Indian Reservation; Augustine Band of Cahuilla Mission Indians of the Augustine Reservation; Cabazon Band of Cahuilla Mission Indians of the Cabazon Reservation; Los Coyotes Band of Cahuilla Mission Indians of the Los Coyotes Reservations; Mornongo Band of Cahuilla Mission Indians of the Mornongo Reservation; Ramona Band or Village of Cahuilla Mission Indians of California; Santa Rosa Band of Cahuilla Mission Indians of Santa Rosa Reservation; Torres-Martinez Band of Cahuilla Mission Indians of California.

Also, Chemehuevi Indian Tribe of the Chemehuevi Reservation; Santa Ynez Band of Chumash Mission Indians of the Santa Ysabel Reservation; Covelo Indian Community of the Round Valley Reservation (Yuki, Pit River, Little Lake, Konkau, Wailaki, Pomo, Nom-Laka, and Wintun Tribes); Barona Group of the Barona Reservation, California; Capitán Grande Band of Diegueño Mission Indians of California; Campo Band of Diegueño Mission Indi-

A Havasupai youngster in Arizona. Because the Havasupai are a federally recognized tribe, this young man is able to gain access to health care and other services that are not available to members of nonrecognized tribes.

ans of the Campo Indian Reservation; Cuyapaipe Community of Diegueño Mission Indians of the Cuyapaipe Reservation.

Also, Inaja Band of Diegueño Mission Indians of the Inaja and Cosmit Reservation; La Posta Band of Diegueño Mission Indians of the La Posta Indian Reservation; Manzanita Band of Diegueño Mission Indians of the Manzanita Reservation; Mesa Grande Band of Diegueño Mission Indians of the Mesa Grande Reservation; Santa Ysabel Band of Diegueño Mission Indians of the Santa Ysabel Reservation; Sycuan Band of Diegueño Mission Indians of California; Viejas Group of the Viejas Reservation; Hoopa Valley Tribe of the Hoopa Valley Reservation.

Also, Karok Tribe of California; La Jolla Band of Luiseño Mission Indians of the La Jolla Reservation; Pala Band of Luiseño Mission Indians of the Pala Reservation; Pauma Band of Luiseño Mission Indians of the Pauma and Yuima Reservation; Pechanga Band of Luiseño Mission Indi-

ans of the Pechanga Reservation; Rincon Band of Luiseño Mission Indians of the Rincon Reservation; Soboba Band of Luiseño Mission Indians of the Soboba Reservation; Twenty-nine Palms Band of Luiseño Mission Indians of California; Mohave Tribe; Colorado River Indian Tribes of the Colorado River Indian Reservation, Arizona, and California (Mojave and Chemehuevi).

Also, Utu Utu Gwaitu Paiute Tribe of the Benton Paiute Reservation; Big Pine Band of Owens Valley Paiute and Shoshone Indians of the Big Pine Reservation; Coyote Valley Band of Pomo Indians of California; Salinan Nation; San Manual Band of Serrano Mission Indians of the San Manual Reservation; San Pasqual General Council; Death Valley Timbi-Sha Shoshone Band of California; Tolowa Nation; Tule River Indian Tribe of the Tule River Reservation; Washoe Tribe of Nevada and California; Yurok Indian Tribe.

Not mentioned are numerous rancherias, colonies, communities, and towns in California that are also federally recognized Indian nations.

Colorado: Southern Ute Indian Tribe of the Southern Ute Reservation; the Ute Mountain Tribe of the Ute Mountain Reservation (Colorado, New Mexico, and Utah).

Connecticut: Nashantucket Pequot Tribe.

Florida: Miccosukee Tribe of Indians of Florida; Seminole Tribe of Florida (Dania, Big Cypress, and Brighton Reservations).

Idaho: Coeur D'Alene Tribe of the Coeur D'Alene Reservation; Kootenai Tribe of Idaho; Nez Perce Tribe of Idaho; Shoshone-Bannock Tribes of the Fort Hall Reservation.

Iowa: Sac and Fox Tribe of the Mississippi.

Kansas: Iowa Tribe of Kansas and Nebraska; Kickapoo Tribe of Indians of the Kickapoo Reservation in Kansas; Prairie Band of Potawatomi Indians of Kansas; Sac and Fox Tribe of Missouri in Kansas and Nebraska.

Louisiana: Chitimacha Tribe of Louisiana; Coushatta Tribe of Louisiana; Tunica-Biloxi Indian Tribe of Louisiana.

Maine: Houlton Band of Maliseet of Maine; Passamaquoddy Tribe of Maine; Penobscot Tribe of Maine.

Massachusetts: Gay Head Wampanoag Indians of Massachusetts.

Michigan: Lac Vieux Desert Band of Lake Superior Chippewa Indians in Michigan; Saginaw Chippewa Indian Tribe of Michigan, Isabella Reservation; Sault Ste. Marie Tribe of Chippewa Indians of Michigan; Grand Traverse Band of Ottawa and Chippewa Indians of Michigan; numerous other federally recognized Indian communities in Michigan.

Minnesota: Minnesota Chippewa Tribe (comprised of six component reservations or bands); Mdewakanton Sioux with four reservations in Minnesota.

Mississippi: Mississippi Band of Choctaw Indians.

Montana: Assiniboine and Sioux Tribes of the Fort Peck Indian Reservation; Blackfeet Tribe of the Blackfeet Indian Reservation of Montana; Chippewa-Cree Indians of the Rocky Boy Reservation; Crow Tribe of Montana; Northern Cheyenne Tribe of the Northern Cheyenne Indian Reservation; Confederated Salish and Kootenai Tribes of the Flathead Reservation.

Nebraska: Omaha Tribe of Nebraska; Santee Sioux Tribe of the Santee Reservation of Nebraska; Winnebago Tribe of Nebraska.

Nevada: Confederated Tribes of the Goshute Reservation, Nevada, and Utah; Duckwater Shoshone Tribe of the Duckwater Reservation; Temoak Tribe of Western Shoshone Indians of Nevada; Constituent Bands of the Temoak Tribe of Western Shoshone Indians; Yomba Shoshone Tribe of the Yomba Reservation; Moapa Bank of Paiute Indians of the Moapa River Indian Reservation; Pyramid Lake Paiute Tribe of the Pyramid Lake Reservation; Summit Lake Paiute Tribe of Nevada; Walker River Paiute Tribe of the Walker River Reservation.

Also, Fort McDermitt Paiute and Shoshone Tribes of the Fort McDermitt Indian Reservation; Shoshone-Paiute Tribes of the Duck Valley Reservation; Paiute-Shoshone Tribe of the Fallon Reservation and Colony; Washoe Tribe; additional colonies, towns, and rancherias.

New Mexico: Jicarilla Apache Tribe of the Jicarilla Apache Indian Reservation; Mescalero Apache Tribe of the Mescalero Reservation; Ramah Navajo Chapter; Pueblos of Acoma, Cochiti, Isleta, Jemez, Laguna, Nambe, Picuris, Pojoaque, San Felipe, San Ildefonso, San Juan, Sandia, Santa Ana, Santa Clara, Santo Domingo, Taos, Tesuque, and Zia; Zuni Tribe of the Zuni Reservation.

New York: Cayuga Nation of New York; St. Regis Band of Mohawk Indians of New York; Oneida Nation of New York; Onondaga Nation of New York; Seneca Nation of New York; Tonawanda Band of Seneca Indians of New York; Tuscarora Nation of New York.

North Carolina: Eastern Band of Cherokee Indians of North Carolina.

North Dakota: Turtle Mountain Band of Chippewa Indians of North Dakota; Three Affil-

Verna Williamson, shown during her term as governor of Isleta Pueblo. Early in the twentieth century, the Pueblo Indians of New Mexico had to sue the United States to gain recognition as Indians. They had been recognized as citizens of Mexico, and the treaty ending the Mexican War in 1848 had declared that all Mexican citizens in territories annexed by the United States automatically became U.S. citizens.

In 1989, relations between the United States and the Onondaga Nation were improved when this ceremony returned twelve wampum belts to the Onondagas. The belts, made of tubular shell beads, are records of tribal history.

iated Tribes of the Fort Berthold Reservation (Mandan, Hidatsa, and Arikara); Devil's Lake Sioux Tribe of the Devil's Lake Sioux Reservation; Standing Rock Sioux Tribe of North and South Dakota.

Oklahoma: Apache Tribe of Oklahoma; Fort Sill Apache Tribe of Oklahoma; Caddo Indian Tribe of Oklahoma; Cherokee Nation of Oklahoma; United Keetoowah Band of Cherokee Indians; Cheyenne-Arapaho Tribes of Oklahoma; Chickasaw Nation of Oklahoma; Choctaw Nation of Oklahoma; Comanche Indian Tribe of Oklahoma; Creek Nation of Oklahoma.

Also, Delaware Tribe of Western Oklahoma; Iowa Tribe of Oklahoma; Kaw Indian Tribe of Oklahoma; Kickapoo Tribe of Oklahoma; Kiowa Indian Tribe of Oklahoma; Miami Tribe of Oklahoma; Modoc Tribe of Oklahoma; Osage Tribe of Oklahoma.

Also, Otoe-Missouria Tribe of Oklahoma; Ottawa Tribe of Oklahoma; Pawnee Indian Tribe of Oklahoma; Peoria Tribe of Oklahoma; Ponca

Tribe of Indians of Oklahoma; Citizen Band Potawatomi Indian Tribe of Oklahoma; Quapaw Tribe of Oklahoma; Sac and Fox Tribe of Oklahoma; Seminole Nation of Oklahoma; Seneca-Cayuga Tribe of Oklahoma; Absentee-Shawnee Tribe of Indians of Oklahoma; Eastern Shawnee Tribe of Oklahoma; Tonkawa Tribe of Oklahoma; Wichita Indian Tribe of Oklahoma; Wyandotte Tribe of Oklahoma; other tribal towns, villages, and communities that are federally recognized.

Oregon: Confederated Tribes of the Umatilla Reservation (Umatilla, Cayuse, and Wallawalla); Coquille Tribe of Oregon; Confederated Tribes of the Grand Ronde Community of Oregon; Klamath Indian Tribe of Oregon; Confederated Tribes of the Siletz Reservation; Cow Creek Band of Umpqua Indians of Oregon; Confederated Tribes of the Warm Springs Reservation of Oregon (Warm Springs, Northern Paiute, and Wasco).

Rhode Island: Narragansett Indian Tribe of Rhode Island.

South Dakota: Cheyenne River Sioux Tribe of the Cheyenne River Reservation; Crow Creek Sioux Tribe of the Crow Creek Reservation; Flandreau Santee Tribe of South Dakota; Lower Brulé Sioux Tribe of the Lower Brulé Reservation; Oglala Sioux Tribe of the Pine Ridge Reservation; Rosebud Sioux Tribe of the Rosebud Indian Reservation; Sisseton-Wahpeton Sioux Tribe of the Lake Traverse Reservation; Standing Rock Sioux Tribe of North and South Dakota; Yankton Sioux Tribe of South Dakota.

Texas: Alabama and Coushatta Tribes of Texas; Kickapoo Traditional Tribe; Ysleta del Sur Pueblo of Texas.

Utah: Skull Valley Band of Goshute Indians of Utah; Paiute Indian Tribe of Utah; Northwestern Band of Shoshone Indians of Utah; Ute Indian Tribe of the Uintah Ouray Reservation.

Washington: Confederated Tribes of the Chehalis Reservation; three communities of Clallam; Confederated Tribes of the Colville Reservation (Colville, Okanogan, Lakes, San Poil, Methow, Nespelem, Entiat, Wenachee, Moses, Nez Perce, and Palouse); Hoh Indian Tribe of the Hoh Indian Reservation; Kalispel Indian Community of the Kalispel Reservation;

Jamestown Klallam Tribe of Washington; Lummi Tribe of the Lummi Reservation; Makah Indian Tribe of the Makah Indian Reservation; Muckleshoot Indian Tribe of the Muckleshoot Reservation; Nisqually Indian Community of the Nisqually Reservation; Nooksack Indian Tribe of Washington.

Also, Puyallup Tribe of the Puyallup Reservation; Quileute Tribe of the Quileute Reservation; Quinault Tribe of the Quinault Reservation; Shoalwater Bay Tribe of the Shoalwater Bay Indian Reservation (Quinault, Chichinook, and Chehalis); Sauk-Suiattle Indian Tribe of Washington; Skokomish Indian Tribe of the Skokomish Reservation; Tulalip Tribes of the Tulalip Reservation; Spokane Tribe of the Spokane Reservation; Squaxin Island Tribe of the Squaxin Island Reservation; Stillaguamish Tribe of Washington; Suquamish Indian Tribe of the Port Madison Reservation; Swinomish Indians of the Swinomish Reservation; Upper Skagit Indian Tribe of Washington; Confederated Tribes of the Bands of the Yakima Indian Nation of the Yakima Reservation.

Wisconsin: Bad River Band of the Lake Superior Tribe of Chippewa Indians of the Bad River Reservation; Lac Courte Oreilles Band of Lake Superior Chippewa Indians of the Lac

The Tulalips are a federally recognized tribe. Here they are shown celebrating the First Salmon Ceremony at the Tulalip Reservation in Washington State. Some Washington tribes, such as the Duwamish, have been denied federal recognition.

Courte Oreilles Reservation of Wisconsin; Lac du Flambeau Band of Lake Superior Chippewa Indians of the Lac du Flambeau Reservation of Wisconsin; Red Cliff Band of Lake Superior Chippewa Indians of Wisconsin; St. Croix Chippewa Indians of Wisconsin, St. Croix Reservation; Menominee Indian Tribe of Wisconsin; Stockbridge-Munsee Community of Mohican Indians of Wisconsin; Wisconsin Winnebago Indian Tribe of Wisconsin.

Wyoming: Arapaho Tribe of the Wind River Reservation; Shoshone Tribe of the Wind Reservation.

This listing of federally recognized nations does not include colonies, rancherias, and tribal towns, even though many are also federally recognized.

— S. S. Davis

SEE ALSO:
Termination Policy; Unrecognized Nations and Tribes.

FEDERATION OF SASKATCHEWAN INDIAN NATIONS

Though the Federation of Saskatchewan Indian Nations (FSIN) has evolved as a Native organization since the 1930s, it was formally founded in its present form in 1982. FSIN's earliest predecessor was the Saskatchewan Treaty Protection Agency, formed in 1930. Its objective was to protect the treaty rights of Indians in the Fort Qu'Appelle area. In the 1940s, this agency became the Protective Association for Indians and Their Treaties. In 1943, the Association of Indians of Saskatchewan was formed.

In 1946, the government of Saskatchewan convened a conference where sixty representatives of the Cree, Saulteaux, Assiniboine, and Sioux tribes passed a resolution forming a single Indian organization. Subsequently, the Union of Saskatchewan Indians, representing all Saskatchewan bands, was formed under the presidency of John Tootoosis.

In 1958, following two conferences of Saskatchewan's chiefs and councilors, the Federation of Saskatchewan Indians (FSI) formed. Dur-

ing the 1970s, FSI reorganized because of the swift pace of internal political development. FSI had been set up as a nonprofit charitable organization under the authority of the province, but this did not conform with its drive for recognition of an Indian government independent of the provincial government. As well, FSI's structure was centralized at the provincial level, rather than at the tribal, council, or band levels, thus removing authority from the tribes.

In 1981, a restructured constitution was adopted in principle. In 1982, the chiefs of the federation tribes agreed to form Canada's first Indian Legislative Assembly. FSI was also restructured to form a true federation of nations, rather than a provincial nonprofit society. The first legislative assembly of the chiefs of Saskatchewan was held on October 19, 1983.

Currently, FSIN includes Cree, Saulteaux, Assiniboine, Dakota-Sioux, and the Dene-Chipewyan Nations. By 1994, there were sixty-nine member bands of FSIN. Each member elects a chief and councilors or headmen to represent their membership.

Ten tribal councils represent the collective interests of groups of bands. For example, the Saskatoon Tribal Council represents seven member bands, while the Prince Albert Tribal Council has twelve member bands. Independent bands that do not belong to any single tribal council are included in the FSIN Convention.

The FSIN members meet on a quarterly basis to discuss policy issues. Its executive consists of one chief, seven vice chiefs, and a regional vice chief. Its executive council includes the executive and tribal council representatives who are elected by their member bands.

Within FSIN are six provincial Native government institutions: the Saskatchewan Indian Federated College, the Saskatchewan Indian Institute of Technologies, the Saskatchewan Indian Cultural College, the Saskatchewan Indian Equity Foundation, the National Indian Financial Corporation, and the Saskatchewan Indian Agricultural Program. There are also over twenty FSIN boards and commissions that deal with issues such as education, economic development, justice, wildlife, government, health, and other concerns.

FEMINISM

The role of women in American Indian society has not been studied extensively by mainstream scholars, and because of the wide variety of Native American societies, no generalizations can be made regarding the aboriginal female role. Women's status generally depended on the economic, social, and religious structures in their communities, with women in some tribes occupying positions involving more power and responsibility than in other tribes. However, women in many different nations have commanded respect within their roles as creators and mothers, cultivators, gatherers, and primary transmitters of culture. Depending upon tribal affiliation, women may also fill roles as healers, religious and political leaders, and even warriors.

One concept that is useful in describing women's power in Native American societies is that of *balanced reciprocity*. While women's roles may have been different from those of men and tasks may have been divided by gender, women and their work were perceived as necessary for the continuation of the society, and a balance of power arose from this perception. The precise status allocated to women often depended on several different aspects of society. For example, matrilineal communities—that is, communities in which family ancestors are traced through the female, rather than male, line—often gave more power to women. Communities that were matrilocal—in which the family lives with or near the wife's mother—also tended to confer more power to women. If a culture's religious traditions include the presence of female deities or icons such as Spider Woman and Corn Maiden, women's roles may also be greater. And societies that were mainly agricultural and that stayed mainly in one place often display more powerful women's roles than the nomadic hunting societies.

The status of Native American women in society has changed throughout history. The impact of colonialism and Christianity upon the role of women has been undeniable: Early contact with Euro-Americans often resulted in the diminishing of the Native American woman's status as the Euro-Americans attempted to reduce her role to equal the relative powerlessness of the Euro-American women. In later contacts, Euro-Americans and others wanted Native American women for stereo-

typed domestic jobs and other "women's work." This brought many Native American women into close contact with the dominant culture, giving them the knowledge necessary to succeed in that society, while the men, stripped of their traditional hunter-warrior roles, remained outsiders. This shifted the balance of power to the female for those participating in the dominant culture.

In the development of the American feminist movement, there is little doubt that such matrilineal Native American societies as the Iroquois provided a model used by the early feminists. In Matilda Joslyn Gage's *Woman, Church and State* (1893), the author acknowledges that "the modern world [is] indebted for its first conception of inherent rights, natural equality of condition, and the establishment of a civilized government upon this basis" to the Iroquois. Gage was probably one of the three most influential feminist architects of the nineteenth-century women's movement, with Elizabeth Cady Stanton and Susan B. Anthony being the others. Knowledge of the Iroquois's matrilineal system of society and government was widespread among early feminists, many of whom lived in upstate New York. The early feminists learned of the Iroquois not only through reading the works of anthropologists and ethnologists such as Lewis H. Morgan, Henry Rowe Schoolcraft, and others, but also through direct personal experience.

With Stanton and Anthony, Gage coauthored the landmark *History of Woman Suffrage,* and in her last book, *Women, Church, and State,* Gage opened with a chapter on "the matriarchate," a form of society she believed existed in a number of early societies, specifically the Iroquois. Gage discussed several Iroquois traditions that tended to create checks and balances between the sexes, including descent through the female line, the ability of women to nominate male leaders, the fact that women had a veto power over decisions to go to war, and the woman's supreme authority in the household. The Iroquois women also had rights to their property and children after divorce. Gage was admitted to the Iroquois Council of Matrons and was adopted into the Wolf Clan with the name *Karonienhawi,* "She Who Holds the Sky."

Native American women have not been noticeably active in the American feminist movement in the United States. Their political activism has con-

These tiles at Plaza de España in Seville, Spain, depict the return of Columbus to the royal court of King Ferdinand and Queen Isabella. When Queen Isabella learned that the five hundred Native people whom Columbus had kidnapped and carried to Spain were being sold in the slave markets of Seville, she ordered them freed and returned to their homes.

centrated on the Native American civil rights movement, and a number of women's organizations came into being to address Indian rights issues. The women's groups were concerned with the continuity and health of their people and with Native cultural preservation; feminism was not a critical issue for them.

Native American women have emerged as contemporary political leaders, with 12 percent of the approximately five nations having female leaders at this time. The most prominent example of a female tribal chairperson is found in Wilma Mankiller, past principal chief of the Cherokee Nation of Oklahoma. The role of Native American women continues to grow and evolve.

— B. E. Johansen / M. A. Stout

SEE ALSO:
Iroquois Confederacy; Mankiller, Wilma.

FERDINAND AND ISABELLA

Ferdinand (1452–1516) and Isabella (1451–1504), joint rulers of Spain, played important roles in defining the nature of contact between Spaniards and the indigenous peoples of the Americas, especially regarding religious intolerance. The marriage of Ferdinand and Isabella united two smaller regions (Aragon and Castile) and created the country of Spain. Ferdinand and Isabella are also known as the *Reyes Catolicos* (the Catholic Kings), because of their religious fanaticism and intolerance. During their reign, the Jews were expelled from Spain, the Spanish Inquisition was begun, and the southern half of Spain was reconquered and taken away from the Muslims. After reconquering Spain and expanding their power, Ferdinand and Isabella extended their power with the exploration and exploitation of the Western Hemisphere.

Ferdinand and Isabella supported Christopher Columbus in his voyages. They considered the voyages to be not only a means of conquering new lands and obtaining wealth, but also an opportunity to expand Christianity.

Ferdinand and Isabella issued many laws and proclamations regarding the treatment of Native peoples. One proclamation required that Indians be given an opportunity to convert to Christianity before they were enslaved. This was considered to be enlightened policy at that time, whereas many Spaniards did not believe that Native people were human. The religious intolerance of the Spanish monarchy did not allow the Native people of the Americas the choice of retaining their Native cultures and religions. Nevertheless, Isabella was concerned that Native people should be better treated. In her will, she pleaded for just treatment of the Indians. The governors of the Spanish provinces in the Americas, while complying with the letter of the law, did not follow its spirit. Under the control of these governors, Indians were abused and enslaved, diseases ravaged their numbers, and nowhere within the Spanish empire were they accorded human dignity and respect.

SEE ALSO:

Catholic Church in the Spanish Empire; Columbian Exchange; Columbus, Christopher; Encomienda; Spain.

FESTIVALS

American Indian festivals are cultural events and celebrations. They are scheduled whenever Indian people decide to come together to celebrate a special observance of some significant event in tribal life. Festivals are usually seasonal and frequently involve feasting.

When Europeans first landed on the North and South American continents, the indigenous people and their traditions were quite diverse, both linguistically and culturally. Much of this diversity

This young Apache girl has won the princess pageant contest and is now marching in the parade at the Apache Tribal Fair in Whiteriver, Arizona.

These young men are participating in the Deer Dance at an annual feast day at San Juan Pueblo in New Mexico. Pueblos in New Mexico have many feast days during the year, and many of them are open to the public.

has been lost as a result of historical encounters with the Europeans. Today, Indian people are finding that many tribes are following similar patterns in reclaiming and recovering their tribal cultures and languages. When Indian people of diverse backgrounds come together, they share certain attributes of life. Festivals provide Indian people opportunities to reclaim and embrace their cultures. Many ceremonies and rituals of diverse Native people are also being brought together in the intertribal powwows, or dances, that are now common across the United States.

All traditional tribal cultures are drawn together by some form of ritual, ceremony, or festival that connects the human spirit. These festivals are astonishingly diverse, ranging from medieval Christian pageants to Mexican Indian dances, from Easter to solstice festivals. They include the annual mask dances found in tribes on the East Coast, the West Coast, and the southern United States, the Sun Dance of the Plains tribes, and the Mide ceremonies of the upper Midwest and Canada. Regardless of the enormous range of rituals and ceremonies, the same traditional Native customs of feasting, chanting, singing, and dancing apply in all of them.

Feasting is a common trait among many festivals throughout the country. From the salmon of the Northwest Coastal tribes to the alligator of the Florida Seminoles to the fry bread of many Oklahoma tribal groups, food permeates most large Indian gatherings. All types of food are brought together for sharing and celebrating.

Traditional festivals are restricted to certain Indian people and their tribal family members, while nontraditional festivals may include many friends and relatives who are both Indians and non-Indians. Many Pueblo feast days invite non-Native people, and so do many intertribal powwows. Usually, traditional festivals are those activities that include only the medicine people of the tribe and those individuals chosen to have a responsible role during the entire event.

For traditional events like the Osage and Pawnee Tail Dance, only the men dance in the sacred circular arena. The Tail Dancers start the traditional Straight Dance ceremony by dancing counterclockwise around the singers, who sit in the middle of the dance arena. For intertribal and social dances, most dancers start out heading clockwise around the singers. This format is referred to as "Southern Style" dancing—referring to those Southern Plains Indian tribes represented in the state of Oklahoma. Tail dancers move their feet downward to greet the earth. A dancer will tell you that he feels the dance within him by listening closely to the drum and styling his dance routine in rhythm with the songs.

Along with dancing, tribal festivals also include chants and songs. These songs are sometimes continuations of mythological cycles or recitations of events that take place in a visionary world. In other cases, songs and chants invoke helping spirits, many times called the "Great Spirit" or "Grandfather." These festivals are often an expression of gratitude for what has been given to Indian people as human beings. Songs and chants are part of a ritual cycle of rhythmic symbolism that reveals man completely interlinked and interconnected with nature, the earth, the sky, and the spirits.

Profoundly bound up with the annual cycles of the seasons, the great ritual cycles of Indian tribal groups are similar to those of other world religions. The annual ceremonial cycles, whether for hunting societies or for agricultural societies, always seek to affirm and augment proper natural conditions. The festive rituals seek to balance or even to intensify the conditions necessary for much wild game or for good crops. They marked the spring and winter cycles—the solstice or equinox—with precise alignments. Although some Indian tribes no longer know the exact ceremonies for which ritual sites were made, still in their alignments we can see how precisely astrological knowledge informed tribal rituals. Indian people observe natural life cycle patterns in order to predict certain events in their lives.

Tribal festivals also include divisions marking the individual life cycle. Rituals marking birth, puberty, maturity, death are only a few special rituals that are often linked to annual or cosmic cycles. For example, a birth might well be celebrated in the spring because of the affiliated celestial and seasonal symbolism of rebirth. Festivals are also linked to the annual cycles of the moon. The moon calendar signifies a rebirth, an annual ritual cycle.

Both the Western view and traditional Indian concepts are introduced in teaching the calendar. Instead of learning the names of twelve months of the year, many Indian children are still introduced to the thirteen moon cycles. Each tribe has its own names for the moon cycles, names that reflect the condition of the natural world and remind Indian people of the activities that should be accomplished.

Many tribes celebrate a New Year festival that represents the birth of the people and of the cosmos. These festivals are essentially world renewal festivals that mark the revitalization of the natural and human worlds. Often marked in part by reverence for ancestors, they sometimes also represent the return of the world from bleakness to fertility or vitality. The New Year is a call for renewed abundant crops, for renewed health among the tribal group, for the blessings of the spirits called upon the earth. For many tribal groups, the New Year festival is also a time for recounting the original creation stories.

Unfortunately, many tribal festivals have been lost. For some time, tribal festivals and rituals were made illegal by the U.S. government, and many traditional men and women had to perform ceremonies and rituals in secret. This secrecy, in turn, meant that sometimes traditional elders could not pass on information about the ceremonies and rituals to younger members of the tribe; therefore, some ceremonies and rituals in many festivals can no longer be properly performed. Sometimes Indian youngsters search for their cultural roots, trying to reconnect and reconstruct some rituals as closely as possible to those once performed by the traditional people of their tribes. But some ceremonies and rituals have been irretrievably lost.

Earth paint is a part of this White Mountain Apache girl's puberty ceremony at the Fort Apache Reservation in Arizona.

Many Indian people see that their traditional ways must be preserved for the next generation. Festivals are significant events central to the tribe's continuation. Modern people sometimes think that ceremonies are but entertainment—a view reinforced by intertribal "shows" and "dancing" for tourists—or that they are merely "superstition." For Indian people, festivals are the form of the mythological and religious cycles that not only make sense of the cosmos, but reveal, augment, and even bring about human beings' harmony with it, and its harmony with them. Without festivals, tribal traditions have no formal expression and cease to exist except as a matter of bloodline and storytelling.

— C. Pewewardy

SEE ALSO:
Calumet Pipe and Dance; Ceremonies, Exploitation of; Creation Stories; Dance, American Indian; Drums; Singing.

FETAL ALCOHOL SYNDROME

Fetal Alcohol Syndrome is a birth disorder that is caused by the harmful consumption of alcohol by mothers during their pregnancies. In the United States, it is currently estimated that full-blown Fetal Alcohol Syndrome (FAS) affects approximately eight thousand babies born per year and that another sixty-five thousand babies are born with varying degrees of Fetal Alcohol Effect (FAE). Exposing a developing fetus to alcohol—even small amounts of alcohol—can create irreversible and serious damage. In severe cases, because the alcohol can go directly into the amniotic fluid that is the baby's environment inside its mother's womb, the baby may suffer the effects of alcohol addiction and even experience withdrawal after it is born. One effect of alcoholism and withdrawal, known as the DTs (delirium tremens), may cause severe trembling, hallucinations, confusion, intense anxiety, and even death.

Babies affected by FAS are often born premature and underweight. They may have grave defects in the bones, heart, brain, and nervous system, as well as visual and hearing impairments. As FAS and FAE babies mature, they may also have a slow-er pattern of growth, become hyperactive and unmanageable, and develop serious learning disabilities. In the years before Fetal Alcohol Syndrome became diagnosed and documented within the medical community, its victims were repeatedly misdiagnosed as having mental retardation or attention deficit disorders. Some were even branded as sociopathic (affected by a personality disorder marked by aggressive, antisocial behavior). Many of them were placed in institutions.

Full-blown Fetal Alcohol Syndrome is more readily distinguishable in infants than is the lesser degree of Fetal Alcohol Effect. Babies born with full-blown FAS may have certain facial characteristics that are similar to the characteristics of some children born with Down Syndrome. They may also have distinct physical and health abnormalities that can be easily recognized as symptomatic of FAS. The symptoms of infants born with Fetal Alcohol Effect (FAE) oftentimes do not appear until the children are much older. Young people with FAE often appear to be perfectly healthy and test in the normal range for intelligence, yet by early adolescence they may begin to reveal unmistakable signs of FAE. These symptoms include comprehension deficits, poor judgment, and behavioral problems such as uncontrollable rages.

The dramatic symptoms of Fetal Alcohol Syndrome and Fetal Alcohol Effect have prompted health professionals to define FAS as America's number-one preventable birth defect. Native American communities are particularly concerned about FAS, because the numbers of Native American babies affected by FAS are alarmingly high—depending on the population sample, between four and twenty-six babies in every one thousand. A book by author Michael Dorris, *The Broken Cord*, estimates that 50 to 80 percent of pregnant women on the Pine Ridge Reservation in South Dakota continue to drink alcohol despite the warnings issued by prenatal clinics. Dorris's book also recounts his family's painful and frustrating struggles with raising an adopted FAS son.

In 1989, Congress passed a law requiring that liquor bottles include warning labels and that bars post signs declaring the hazards of drinking during pregnancy. This has proved valuable and worthwhile in deterring some pregnant mothers from consuming alcohol.

SEE ALSO:
Alcoholism; "Firewater."

SUGGESTED READING:
Dorris, Michael. *The Broken Cord*. New York: Harper and Row, 1989.

"FIREWATER"

The term *firewater*, which refers to alcohol, whiskey, or liquor, is an expression that carries associations with stereotypes of American Indians. It "goes down the throat like fire" was supposedly a response of some Indians upon being introduced to alcohol, and thus the term *firewater* came into being. Exactly when and where the expression originated is unknown, but versions of the term may have appeared as early as the late 1400s or early 1500s, when the first Europeans stepped onto North American soil. Though the term may have legitimate origins, it has, like such terms as *squaw*, *papoose*, or *wampum*, become a cliché through its overuse and misapplication to Native people. Thanks to the movies and other popular media, certain expressions that are characteristic of specific Native cultures at specific historical times have been treated as if they apply to all Native cultures throughout the entire era of post-European contact.

Alcohol was introduced to Native Americans by non-Native fur traders and frontiersmen, and it was served by U.S. representatives at treaty councils. Fermented beverages were not unknown among the Native peoples of North America before contact with Europeans, but they were rarely abused and were not produced in large quantities.

Alcohol was called many different things among many different tribes. Among the Sioux, for instance, liquor was sometimes called *mni wakan*, meaning "holy water" or "sacred water." This might have been because the intoxicating effect of alcohol could be likened to a mystical or religious experience. Among the Mohawks, alcohol was sometimes referred to as *deganigohadaynyohs*, meaning "the mind changer." Among the Stoney Nakotas from Canada, alcohol was *gahtonejabee meenee*. The word *gahtonejabee* translates to "drunk," and *meenee*, like *mni*, means "water." Essentially, it meant "crazy

water," or the "water that makes you go crazy." For some Ojibwes, alcohol was called *skwidayabo*, meaning "firewater." Other translated terms for alcohol were "bad water," "white-man's water," or "poison water." Whatever the term for alcohol, its introduction to Indian communities has had a serious and damaging effect on the health and well-being of those communites. Today, the debilitating effect of alcohol is a problem faced by tribal governments and Native health officials everywhere.

SEE ALSO:
Alcoholism; Fetal Alcohol Syndrome.

FIRST AMENDMENT

The First Amendment to the United States Constitution recognizes the right of all Americans to think, worship, and speak freely: "Congress shall make no law respecting an establishment of religion, or prohibiting the free exercise thereof; or abridging the freedom of speech, or of the press, or the right of the people peaceably to assemble, and to petition the Government for a redress of grievances."

Despite Thomas Jefferson's description of a bill of rights as "what the people are entitled to against every government on earth," the First Amendment and remaining provisions in the Bill of Rights (the first fourteen amendments to the U.S. Constitution) were not originally intended to apply to Native Americans, or to African slaves in the South, at the time of ratification on December 15, 1791. The federal Civil Rights Act of 1866 extended "full and equal benefit of all laws and proceedings" to slaves freed as a result of the U.S. Civil War, but the act specifically excluded American Indians. The Bill of Rights has only recently become a real source of protection for Native Americans.

It is important to note that the constitutional guarantees in the Bill of Rights did not actually protect *most* Americans until the early years of the twentieth century, when the courts first began to hear legal challenges to violations of individual rights. Prior to this time, most Americans were relatively uninformed about their rights and lacked access to the legal and financial resources necessary to pursue remedies for violations of their rights.

In 1919, the U.S. Supreme Court heard its first case involving a First Amendment concern fully 130 years after the Bill of Rights was ratified. Since that time, cases involving American Indian concerns about free speech or religious freedom have always been few in number.

First Amendment protections for Native people have been extended only within the last thirty years and have largely been the result of rulings not directly related to Native Americans. For example, in 1969, the Supreme Court ruled in *Tinker v. Des Moines* that "symbolic speech" was protected under the First Amendment. Although the facts of the case involved students wearing black armbands to protest the Vietnam War, this ruling opened the door for American Indians to challenge the prohibition of sacred articles, such as eagle feathers, in many states.

Native Americans have also used the First Amendment to pursue judicial and legislative action to expand legal protection for various forms of Native religious worship, including the use of peyote for ceremonial purposes. The American Indian Religious Freedom Act (AIRFA) was passed in 1978 and formally extended the guarantees of the First Amendment's "Establishment Clause" to Native Americans. (The establishment clause is the common name for the first portion of the First Amendment, which says that "Congress shall make no law respecting an establishment of religion.")

Even AIRFA has been subject to judicial review, and recently the Supreme Court has sought to limit its scope. For example, in 1988, the Supreme Court held that sacred sites deserved no protection, and in 1990, it refused to recognize peyote as an integral part of Native American Church practices. As a result of Native lobbying efforts, however, Congress passed and President Clinton signed the Peyote Bill in 1994, once again recognizing religious freedom for Indians.

In addition to asserting their rights to use peyote in ceremonies, protect sacred sites from development or commercial use, and possess religious articles, Native Americans have also used the First Amendment to fight for the right of prisoners to see traditional spiritual leaders and practice Native

forms of worship. These struggles are ongoing as interpretations of the First Amendment, now over two hundred years old, continue to evolve.

SEE ALSO:

Franklin, Benjamin; Constitution, United States; Iroquois Confederacy; Jefferson, Thomas; Noble Savage.

FIRST BOOK AWARDS

The First Book Awards are a publication and prize competition for beginning and emerging Native American literary writers. Authors of the winning manuscripts receive a five-hundred-dollar prize and publication of their booklength manuscript by a participating press. Authors also receive travel expenses to an awards banquet held in July of each year at the University of Oklahoma, where the annual Lifetime Achievement Award of the

Anishinabe (Ojibwe) poet Kimberly Blaeser won the First Book Award in poetry in 1993 for a collection of poems titled *Trailing You*.

Hunkpapa Sioux poet Tiffany Midge won the First Book Award in poetry in 1994 for a collection of poems titled *Outlaws, Renegades, and Saints: Diary of a Mixed-up Halfbreed.*

Native Writers' Circle of the Americas is also presented.

The First Book Awards were inaugurated in 1992 in conjunction with the Returning the Gift festival of North American Native literary writers at the University of Oklahoma. The competition is sponsored and administered by the Native Writers' Circle of the Americas, which is a professional Native literary writers' organization, and the Greenfield Review Press of Greenfield Center, New York. In 1992, the First Book Awards were offered in four categories: poetry, prose, creative nonfiction, and drama. Since then, two awards, in poetry and prose, have been made each year.

In 1992, the First Book Awards were as follows: the Diane Decorah Memorial Award for Poetry was shared by Joe Dale Tate Nevaquaya (Yuchi-

Comanche) for *Leaving Holes* and by Gloria Bird (Spokane) for *Moon Over the Reservation;* the Louis Littlecoon Oliver Memorial Award for Short Fiction was presented to Robert Perea (Oglala Sioux) for *Stacey's Story;* the Richard Margolis Memorial Award for Creative Nonfiction was presented to Melissa Fawcett Sayett (Mohegan) for *The Lasting of the Mohegans;* and the Drama Award was presented to William S. Yellow Robe, Jr. (Assiniboine), for *The Star Quilter.*

In 1993, the Diane Decorah Memorial Award for Poetry was won by Kimberly Blaeser (White Earth Anishinabe) for *Trailing You,* and the Louis Littlecoon Oliver Memorial Prose Award was won by Philip H. Red-Eagle (Sisseton-Wahpeton-Klallam) for *Red Earth: Native American Experiences in Vietnam.* In 1994, the Diane Decorah Memorial Award for Poetry was won by Tiffany Maria Midge (Hunkpapa Sioux) for *Diary of a Mixed-up Halfbreed,* and the Louis Littlecoon Oliver Memorial Prose Award was won by Gus Palmer, Jr.(Kiowa), for *Calling Through the Creek.* In 1995, the Diane Decorah Memorial Award for Poetry was won by Denise H. Sweet (White Earth Anishinabe) for *Songs for Discharming,* and the Louis Littlecoon Oliver Memorial Prose Award was won by Glenn J. Twist (Cherokee-Muscogee) for *Boston Mountain Tales.*

Competition for the First Book Awards is restricted to authors of provable Native American descent who have not yet published a first book. In general, poetry manuscripts submitted in the competition must be between 48 and 100 pages, single-spaced, and prose manuscripts must be between 120 pages and 240 pages, double-spaced. There is no entry fee, and authors may submit no more than one manuscript in each category. Annual deadline for the submission of manuscripts is the first of May. All entries must be accompanied with a preaddressed return mailer and sufficient postage for the return of the manuscript. The rules are subject to variation year by year, and there are other rules not mentioned here. Current rules of the competition may be obtained from First Book Awards, The Greenfield Review Press, P.O. Box 308, Greenfield Center, NY 12833.

SEE ALSO:
Returning the Gift.

FIRST SALMON CEREMONY

Native peoples across North America customarily honored their main food source with events like the First Salmon Ceremony of the Pacific Northwest. All along the Northwest Coast, the first catch of salmon in the late summer and early fall runs was laid along a riverbank, often with their heads pointed upstream, sometimes on a woven mat or cedar board. Sometimes a special shelter was constructed for the first salmon to be caught.

The first catch might be sprinkled with birds' down, as a formal speech of welcome was given: "Oh, friends! Thank you that we meet alive. We have lived until this time when you came this year. Now we pray you, Supernatural Ones, to protect us from danger, that nothing evil may happen to us when we eat you, Supernatural Ones! For that is the reason why you come here, that we may catch you for food. We know that only your bodies are dead here, but your souls come to watch over us when we are going to eat what you have given us."

The people assembled around the fish responded "Indeed" as the body of it was cooked and divided among them in small portions. Such ceremonies might last for several days of feasting and gift giving, as large numbers of migrating salmon were allowed past the Indians' nets to ensure the continuation of the salmon runs. Then fishing resumed.

Many Native peoples who subsisted mainly on salmon runs intentionally let the fish pass after they had taken enough to see them through the year. They were acting through conscious knowledge that the salmon runs would vanish if too few fish escaped their nets to reach spawning grounds at the headwaters of rivers and streams.

In Northwest Native tradition, the salmon are believed to host spirit beings who have their village out under the western ocean. Those Indians who visited them in visions saw them living in great houses like human beings. Their annual pilgrimages to the mountain streams was seen as a voluntary sacrifice for the benefit of their human friends. Though they seemed to die, the spirits had simply

The First Salmon Ceremony is an important event to Native peoples throughout the Pacific Northwest. Here the Tulalips celebrate the First Salmon Ceremony on the Tulalip Reservation in Washington State.

removed their outer "salmon robes" and journeyed back to their undersea homes. They would return again only if their gifts of flesh were treated with careful respect.

SEE ALSO:
Fishing Rights.

FISHING RIGHTS

When the Romans colonized Gaul about the time of the birth of Christ, they found a fish-eating people. Soon the demand for the pink-fleshed fish they named *salmo,* "the climber," rose in Roman markets. The waters were overfished, stocks were depleted, and in the ensuing centuries, the salmon became extinct in many European rivers.

The taste for salmon traveled with the European colonists to the Americas; by the turn of the century, the descendants of the fishermen who had feasted on salmon in Europe, before cattle and sheep were domesticated, found the same fish in many streams of the Pacific Northwest. In that area and time, it was said, one could walk across the backs of the salmon from one stream bank to another. Fifty thousand Indians took 18 million pounds (8 million kilograms) of salmon a year from the Columbia River watershed before civilization began to deplete the runs.

To the Northwest Indian nations, the salmon was as central to economic life as the buffalo on the Plains; 80 to 90 percent of the Puyallup diet, for example, was fish. The salmon was more than food; it was the center of a way of life. A cultural festival accompanied the first salmon caught in the yearly run. The fish was barbecued over an open fire and bits of its flesh parceled out to all. The bones were saved intact, to be carried by a torchbearing, singing, dancing, and chanting procession back to the river. There they were placed into the water, the head pointed upstream, symbolic of the spawning fish, so the run would return in later years.

Ojibwe (Chippewa or Anishinabe) spearfishers in 1990 at Lac du Flambeau, Wisconsin, prepare to engage in the annual ancient fishing practices of their ancestors. Their right to practice traditional methods of fishing has been guaranteed by treaties and upheld in the federal courts, despite violent protests by non-Indians.

This Yakima tribal member is dip-net fishing for chinook salmon in the Klickitat River, a tributary of the Columbia River in the south-central portion of Washington State.

Lac du Flambeau Ojibwe (Chippewa) spearfishers push off from a landing in defiance of antispearing protesters during a 1989 dispute over Native fishing rights in Wisconsin.

Washington became a territory of the United States on March 2, 1853, with no consent from the Indians who occupied most of the land. Isaac Stevens was appointed governor and superintendent of Indian affairs for the territory. As governor, Stevens wished to build the economic base of the territory; this required the attraction of a proposed transcontinental railroad, which, in turn, required peace with the Indians. Stevens worked with remarkable speed; in 1854 and 1855 alone, he negotiated five treaties with six thousand Indian people west of the Cascades. By signing the treaties, the Indians ceded to the United States 2,240,000 acres (896,000 hectares) of land, an immense sacrifice for the right to fish.

Around 1914, 16 million fish were caught annually; by the 1920s, annual catches had declined to an average of 6 million. In the late 1930s, following construction of several large hydroelectric dams on the Columbia River and its tributaries, the annual catch had fallen as low as 3 million, about one-sixth of what Native peoples

alone had been harvesting a century earlier. By the 1970s, with more aggressive conservation measures in place, including construction of fish ladders at most major dams, the annual catch had risen to 4 to 6 million, just short of a third of the precontact harvest.

Native peoples who had signed the Medicine Creek Treaty and other nineteenth-century treaties were having a more difficult time harvesting enough fish to survive, even though the treaty gave them the right to fish as long as the rivers run. By the early 1960s, however, in disregard of treaties granting Indians the right to fish beyond the limits granted non-Natives, state fisheries police were conducting wholesale arrests of Indians, confiscating their boats and nets. Denied justice in the state courts, the tribes pursued their claim at the federal level. During the 1960s and early 1970s, they also militantly protected their rights in the face of raids by state fisheries authorities. A nucleus of fishing-rights activists from Franks Landing, living only a few miles (kilometers) from the site at which the Medicine Creek Treaty had been signed, continued to fish on the basis of that treaty.

The fish-ins continued until February 12, 1974, when U.S. District Court Judge George Boldt ruled that Indians were entitled to an opportunity to catch as many as half the fish returning to off-reservation sites that had been the "usual and accustomed places" when the treaties were signed. State officials and the fishermen whose interests they represented were furious at Boldt. Rumors circulated about the sanity of the seventy-five-year-old judge. It was said that he had taken bribes of free fish and had an Indian mistress, neither of which was true. Judge Boldt was hung in effigy by angry non-Indian fishermen. On other occasions, they formed "convoys" with their boats and rammed U.S. Coast Guard vessels that had been dispatched to enforce the court's orders regarding the Indians' retaining their right to fish. At least one coastguardsman was shot.

A backlash to Indian rights formed among state officials during the middle and late 1970s, a backlash that would become the nucleus for a nationwide non-Indian campaign to abrogate the treaties. Washington State Attorney General (later U.S. Senator) Slade Gorton called Indians "supercitizens" with "special rights" and proposed that constitutional equilibrium be reestablished not by the state's openly violating the treaties (Boldt had outlawed that), but by purchasing the Indians' fishing rights. The tribes, which had been listening to offers of money for Indian resources for a century, flatly refused Gorton's offer. To them, the selling of fishing rights would have been tantamount to termination of their tribal status and Native identity.

In the early 1980s, fishing rights became a national movement, as the Ojibwes (Chippewas) began to reassert their aboriginal rights to hunt, fish, and gather in areas specified in their treaties negotiated in the nineteenth century. This reasser-

In 1990 in Polk County, Wisconsin, Ojibwe spearfishers stand on top of a picnic table to gain an advantage over antispearing protesters at a boat landing at Cedar Lake.

tion of treaty rights resulted in legal disputes. On January 25, 1983, the U.S. Court of Appeals for the Seventh Circuit agreed with the Lake Superior Chippewa that hunting, fishing, and gathering rights were still reserved and protected in Chippewa treaties. This was known as the Voigt decision. Later, the United States Supreme Court refused to hear the appeal of the Voigt decision by the state of Wisconsin, thus affirming the ruling of the seventh circuit. However, the three-judge panel of the seventh circuit did return the case to federal district court to "determine the scope of state regulation." Subsequent decisions defined the scope of Chippewa hunting, fishing, and gathering rights in Wisconsin so that they have the right to harvest and sell hunting, fishing, and gathering products; to exercise these rights on private land if necessary to produce a modest living; and to harvest a quantity sufficient to produce a modest living.

— B. E. Johansen

SEE ALSO:
Boldt, George Hugo; Bressette, Walter; Ecology, Native American Conceptions of; Lummi; Ojibwe.

FIVE CIVILIZED TRIBES

The so-called Five Civilized Tribes consisted of three Muskhogean language-family members (Chickasaws, Choctaws, and Seminoles), one confederation of tribes whose members are predominantly Muskhogean speaking (the Muscogee Confederation, also known as Creeks), and one tribe from the Iroquoian language family (Cherokees). For many generations before European contact, the ancestral homelands of the Choctaws, Chickasaws, and Creeks were in the southeastern portion of the North American continent. The Cherokees had also been living in this region for generations before European contact but had apparently migrated there from the lands of their Iroquoian-speaking relatives in the north at some time in the distant past. The Seminoles separated from the Creeks and developed an independent tribal identity after the arrival of Europeans.

From earliest contact, Europeans were impressed with the agricultural capabilities of these nations, their military prowess, their orderly towns, and the poise with which they conducted their public affairs.

Seals of the Five Civilized Tribes, whose lands occupy the eastern portion of the present state of Oklahoma.

A photo of Seminoles in the Florida Everglades, visited in 1928 by H. B. Collins, an archaeologist of the Smithsonian Institution.

The newcomers admired the Natives' extensive intertribal trading networks and their interest in and adaptability to European cultural ideas and objects. A vigorous trade developed between European colonial nations and tribes in the Southeast, which soon led to an intense rivalry between Europeans for trade monopolies with individual tribes. With French, English, and Spanish colonial presences in the Southeast all competing against each other, the tribes soon displayed diplomatic skills in dealing with the Europeans, wringing concessions from them that often exasperated Europeans, while winning their respect. Maintaining a trade monopoly with a tribe soon became an expensive undertaking requiring substantial outlays of capital in the form of gifts to tribal leaders, which they, in turn, redistributed to their people.

By the time the English colonies had gained their independence, established the United States government, and survived the War of 1812 with England, a number of whites had intermarried within the southeastern tribes and produced mixed-blood offspring. The tribes increasingly looked to these offspring to deal with the United States. Mixed-blood families, loyal to their tribe, were also influential in spreading many European-American cultural influences throughout their tribes. Educational systems were organized with the help of missionaries, printed alphabets and grammars were developed, books were published in Native languages, and European-style clothing gained popularity. Among the Cherokees, Sequoyah developed a Cherokee syllabary that allowed virtually the whole nation to become literate within only a few years.

Among the Choctaws, by 1824 James Lawrence McDonald had been educated and admitted to the bar. This lawyer proved to be an effective negotiator in treaties with the United States. Throughout the early decades of the nineteenth century, Americans became increasingly aware that southeastern tribes rivaled white settlers in the region in the characteristics that were associated with "civilized" life.

The Choctaw Nation Tribal Complex is located in Durant, Oklahoma, in a building that originally housed the Oklahoma Presbyterian College For Women.

The Five Civilized Tribes displayed economic, political, and social attributes that were valued by the whites, causing a moral dilemma for some Americans in the 1830s when the United States sought to wrest all of the tribes' homelands from them and remove them west of the Mississippi River. In 1838, Ralph Waldo Emerson wrote a letter to President Martin Van Buren, protesting the imminent removal of the Cherokees and citing their many accomplishments. These protests, however, could not forestall removal.

For all of the tribes, removal from their ancestral homelands was a bitter experience that caused the death of thousands of people. Once arrived in the West, however, the tribes recovered from the trauma of removal, adopted written constitutions, created republican governments, and established systems of public education. Within a generation, they had reestablished themselves as vigorous thriving nations.

The U.S. Civil War, 1861 to 1865, wrecked their Native economies and produced chaos within their nations for the duration of the war. The United States, obligated by treaties to provide military protection to the tribes, abandoned them entirely at the outbreak of the war; it withdrew all federal troops from the region and left them to deal with the Confederacy on their own. In the northern half of Indian Territory, in the Cherokee and Creek Nations, the Native people saw their land turned into battlefields, while in the southern half of the territory, floods of refugees from the northern half of the territory created food shortages within the Choctaw and Chickasaw Nations.

At the conclusion of the Civil War, the United States punished the Indian nations in Indian Territory for entering into diplomatic relations with the Confederacy by exacting concessions from the nations for railway construction through their lands. This soon led to a stream of non-Indian immigration that, by the end of the century, overwhelmed the Native peoples in their own nations.

Late in the nineteenth century, the Congress forced the tribes to accept individual allotments of land from the tribal estate. It then sold the remaining land to settlers. With the creation of the state of Oklahoma in 1907, Congress declared that the Indian nations in Indian Territory no longer existed.

Throughout the twentieth century, the United States government policy toward the Native peoples of Oklahoma has alternated between policies that could help them regain some measure of tribal sovereignty and self-determination and policies of attempting to terminate relations between Indian nations and the United States. Finally, in the 1970s, legislation was enacted that enabled the tribes to reform their governments, write new constitutions, and develop and administer many social and health programs for their people. Today, each of the five tribes maintains a modern tribal headquarters complex, employs many people in tribal operations, and administers health clinics, hospitals, business enterprises, gaming facilities, home construction programs, and law enforcement services. Their numbers are growing as more and more displaced tribal members are enrolled, with the two largest tribes being the Cherokees with more than 150,000 members and the Choctaws with nearly 100,000 members.

In the ancestral homelands east of the Mississippi River, some Native peoples avoided removal. Today, there are federally recognized tribal governments of Choctaws in Mississippi, Seminoles in Florida, and Cherokees in North Carolina. In addition, there are other communities of Creeks in Alabama and Georgia and Choctaws in Alabama and Louisiana.

— D. L. Birchfield

SEE ALSO:

Cherokee; Chickasaw; Choctaw; Creek; Seminole.

SUGGESTED READINGS:

Cotterill, R. S. *The Southern Indians: The Story of the Five Civilized Tribes Before Removal.* Norman: University of Oklahoma Press, 1954.

Foreman, Grant. *The Five Civilized Tribes.* Norman: University of Oklahoma Press, 1934.

Wright, Muriel H. *A Guide to the Indian Tribes of Oklahoma.* Norman: University of Oklahoma Press, 1951.

FIVE NATIONS

SEE Iroquois Confederacy.

FIXICO, DONALD L. (1951–)

Donald L. Fixico is an American Indian historian and professor of American Indian studies. He is of Creek, Seminole, Sac and Fox, and Shawnee heritage. He earned a Ph.D. degree from the University of Oklahoma and has taught at the University of Oklahoma, the University of California at Los Angeles, the University of Wisconsin–Milwaukee, and Western Michigan University.

His doctoral dissertation is entitled *Termination and Relocation: Federal Indian Policy, 1945–1960.* It is primarily a history of federal Indian policy during the 1950s. Fixico is currently working on a book entitled *Indian America in the Twentieth Century.* He has served on the editorial advisory board of a number of scholarly journals, including the *American Indian Culture and Research Journal,* published by the American Indian Studies Center of the University of California at Los Angeles, and the *Native Press Research Journal,* published by the American Native Press Archives at the University of Arkansas at Little Rock.

He has described the concept of "parallel coexistence" regarding today's American Indian tribes on reservations and the efforts to improve conditions with regards to the future direction of federal Indian policy and the criticism directed toward Indian treaty rights.

Fixico's other writings on American Indian history include works on the Muskogee Creeks and on the relation between tribal leaders and the demand for natural resources on reservation lands.

FLOOD, STORY OF

SEE Creation Stories.

FLORIDA

Florida, which became a U.S. state in 1845, received its name in 1513 from Juan Ponce de León, a Spanish explorer who was amazed by all of the flowers and other lush plant life he saw and named the land *Florida,* a Spanish word meaning "full of flowers."

Miccosukee Seminole children at play at a camp in the Florida Everglades.

At the time of European contact, four major Indian groups lived in Florida: the Apalachees, in the northwest; the Timucas, in the central portion; the Tequestas, in the southeast; and the Calusas, in the southwest. The four groups had a total population of one hundred thousand to nine hundred thousand. Diseases introduced into the population from Europe, Spanish slave raiding, and warfare almost entirely wiped out these Native cultures.

In the 1700s, two Indian tribes migrated to Florida. In about 1700, the Seminole people separated from the Creek tribe in order to live independently in Florida. In the second decade of the eighteenth century, after the Yamasee War, 1715–1716, the Yamasee tribe was driven southward and was assimilated into the Seminole tribe.

During the 1700s and early 1800s, many escaped slaves found refuge with the Seminole people. Because of their long-standing conflict with Europeans and non-Native Americans—and because of their refusal to return escaped slaves—the Seminoles were drawn into the First Seminole War,

1817–1818. That war ended in a treaty, but the Second Seminole War raged from 1835–1842. In 1842, 4,000 of the 4,300 Seminoles surrendered and were moved to the Indian Territory in Oklahoma. The three hundred Seminoles who refused to surrender remained in the Florida Everglades. No second treaty was ever signed, and so the Seminole technically remained in a state of war against the United States. Currently about 4,000 Seminoles remain in Oklahoma and about 1,500 in Florida.

Florida has an overall Native population of 36,335, placing it fifteenth among U.S. states in American Indian population. Four reservations exist in Florida: Big Cypress—42,728 acres (17,091 hectares) and a population of 447; Brighton—35,805 acres (14,322 hectares) and a population of 402; Hollywood—481 acres (192 hectares) and a population of 484; and Miccosukee—75,146 acres (30,058 hectares) and a population of 94.

SEE ALSO:
Creek; Florida, Indians of; Seminole.

FLORIDA, INDIANS OF

The Indian people of the state of Florida were very unusual because of their racial blend. Those Indians who first lived in the state—the Apalachee, the Timuca, the Tequesta, and the Calusa—were completely wiped out by disease and by warfare with the Spanish. In the 1700s, the Yamasee and the Seminoles—who had branched off from the Creeks and considered their former tribe enemies—moved into Florida.

Some of the Seminoles were of mixed Indian and white blood. In the decades that followed, many Blacks joined the tribe through marriage and as slaves. The Seminole Black slaves held an unusual position in the tribe. Although they were not considered to be full members of the tribe, they were allowed to live freely and to carry weapons. The mixed-blood Seminoles who were part Indian and part Black were considered to be full members of the tribe. Out of fourteen hundred Black Seminoles, only two hundred were claimed as slaves. The Seminoles defended their Black tribal members and slaves against slave raiders and killed those slave hunters who ventured into their territory.

In 1817, the First Seminole War began when General Andrew Jackson attacked northern Florida to punish the Seminoles and to seize runaway slaves. The first Seminole War ended in a treaty after almost no action as the Seminoles simply kept avoiding Jackson and his men.

The Second Seminole War began soon after many of the Seminole chiefs refused to sign the Treaty of Payne's Landing. If the Seminoles agreed to the treaty, they would be removed to the Creek Reservation in Oklahoma and they would receive $15,400 for all their Florida lands. Each Seminole would also receive "one blanket and one homespun frock." Of the monies that the tribe received, they were to pay $7,000 in damages for not returning runaway slaves. At the time of the treaty, slave hunters were seizing runaway slaves, mixed-blood Seminoles, and full-blood Seminoles and selling them into slavery in Georgia and the Carolinas.

Osceola was among those most adamant in their opposition to the treaty. Although he was not a

A contemporary lithograph of Seminoles in Florida in 1840 responding to attacks upon them by the U.S. Army in the long and bloody war waged by the United States against the Seminole people.

A Seminole medicine man in Florida performing a ritual for the benefit of his people.

Seminole tribal members displaying traditional Seminole dress in Tampa, Florida.

chief, many Seminoles followed him because of his personality and strength of character. Osceola was known as "Powell" to whites and was rumored to be half white, perhaps because it bothered the whites to be beaten by an Indian. When Osceola refused to sign the treaty, he was arrested and placed in irons. He recanted and agreed to sign, but as soon as he was released, he gathered other dissidents and fled.

Osceola's strategy was simple. He intended to avoid superior forces while he constantly raided and harassed the enemy. On December 28, 1835, Osceola and his men wiped out all but three members of a one-hundred-man force that was sent against him. On the same day, he also killed the general, Wiley Thompson, who had tried to force him to sign the treaty. Osceola continued his strategy and deviated only one time when he entered into a pitched battle at a ford on the Ouithlacoochee River. In the battle, he was wounded and lost some warriors, but he and his men killed or wounded sixty-three United States soldiers.

A new commander, General Thomas Sidney Jesup, took the field in Florida and attempted to get the Seminoles to enter into a peace treaty. When he failed in this, he was subjected to Osceola's raids, which caused him great frustration. The U.S. government sent him one thousand Shawnee, Delaware, and Kickapoo fighting men with the idea that Indians could hunt down other Indians even if white men could not. These Indians did not prove to be very successful since they did not know the swamps the way the Seminoles did.

On October 21, 1837, Jesup enacted another plan. He seized Osceola and seventy-five of his warriors when they agreed to meet with him for a peace discussion. Osceola died three months later in prison at Fort Moultrie, near Charleston. The Seminole leader Coacoochee, known as "Wild Cat," and twenty other warriors escaped from prison and resumed fighting.

Many congressmen and other Americans were appalled at Jesup's deceit, and he was replaced by Colonel Zachary Taylor as commander. On December 25, 1837, Taylor and a body of 600 soldiers attacked a Seminole village on Lake Kissimmee. After hard fighting, Taylor and his troops pushed the Seminoles back, but at a cost of 28 dead and 111 wounded.

Taylor was replaced by General William J. Worth, a hero of the War of 1812 and a former commandant of West Point Military Academy. Worth was successful where others had not been because he systematically destroyed Seminole villages and fields and weakened the Seminoles with hunger.

Finally, in 1842, four thousand Seminoles surrendered and were sent to Oklahoma. Three hundred Seminoles refused to leave Florida, and their descendants still live in the Everglades. Some of these Florida Seminoles refused to be drafted during World War II, stating that they were not United States citizens, but members of the independent Seminole Nation.

The Seminoles who moved to Oklahoma encountered more troubles. The Black Seminoles set up a town, called Wewoka, which the Creeks attacked. Comanches wiped out another party of mixed-blood Seminoles. Under the Black Seminole leader, John Horse, about two hundred Black Seminoles fled to Mexico, where they offered their services as soldiers to the Mexican government.

The mixed-blood Seminoles were very successful in that service, and other Black Seminoles were active as United States Army scouts during Indian wars in the Southwest. Approximately four thousand Seminoles remain in Oklahoma today, and about fifteen hundred remain in Florida.

— T. Colonnese

SEE ALSO:
Five Civilized Tribes; Florida; Jackson, Andrew; Osceola; Seminole.

FLUTE, NATIVE AMERICAN

The Native American flute is an ingeniously designed musical instrument. To produce a tone on some flutes, one blows across a hole or into a mouthpiece that directs the air across a notch. In the Native American flute, air enters a small hole at the top of the instrument. An inner partition directs the air up and out of the flute. However, the air is then directed across the top of the partition and against a metal lip by a boxlike structure known as a "saddle." The airflow is split by this lip. Part of the air reenters the long lower chamber of the flute, while part escapes. Splitting the air causes the air column in the rest of the instrument to vibrate. Covering the finger holes on the flute changes the length of the vibrating column, thus changing the pitch. Traditionally, such flutes were widespread in North America south of Canada.

According to many tribal sources, the traditional use of the flute was by men for courtship, for personal enjoyment, and for entertaining friends and visitors. Though the instrument is often called a courting flute, many Native groups, such as the Lenape and other East Coast tribes, probably did not use it for courtship.

While the flute remained the same in principal across North America, there was great variation in its length, the dimensions of its interior, and the number of finger holes. Tuning techniques therefore varied from group to group, although each group probably had its own general tuning system.

The flutes were constructed differently according to the groups to which they belonged. Among some groups, wood was split, each piece was hollowed out, and the pieces were reassembled. Flute makers in other groups hollowed out a piece of wood and added the partition by inserting a plug into the tube. Perhaps the greatest variation occurred in the shape of the saddle. That part of the flute was carved by the player, but within a tradition unique to the player's group.

The flute was a highly personal instrument, and thus each player usually made his own instrument. Many of the songs played on the flute were also highly personal, and each song in turn would be "owned" by the individual player. Native American musicians now play songs of all styles and cultural backgrounds on the flute.

SEE ALSO:
Courting Flute.

FOLSOM CULTURE

In 1927, an African-American cowboy named George McJunkin, working on a ranch in northeastern New Mexico near Folsom, made a discovery that shook the world of archaeology. At a place called Dead Horse Gulch, McJunkin saw some large bones sticking out of the gulch wall, fifteen to twenty feet (four to six meters) beneath the surface of the ground. McJunkin knew that some people were looking for such sites and that J. D. Figgins, a paleontologist from the Denver Museum of Natural History, had contacted ranchers in the area asking that they be on the lookout for them. McJunkin reported what he had found, and when Figgins came to investigate, hoping to find an extinct species of bison, he found much more than that. He found chipped spear points near extinct bison bones estimated to be at least ten thousand years old. The spear points clearly had been made by humans.

The discovery caused archaeologists to rethink everything that they thought they knew about how long humans had been living in the Western Hemisphere. Until the discovery of the Folsom site, archaeologists believed that humans had not been in North America for more than about three or four thousand years. Archaeologists scoffed at Native American oral traditions that told of a much longer tenure on the continent and disregarded their stories about giants—animals much larger than any modern North American animals. People schooled in European methods of inquiry, whether they be archaeologists or historians, have never considered Native oral traditions to be of much interest or usefulness to anyone but anthropologists.

But here, in Folsom, New Mexico, was evidence that archaeologists could not ignore. If humans could be shown to have been on the continent at least ten thousand years ago, then how much longer before that had they been here? It's a question that archaeologists have been debating and searching out answers for ever since the discovery of what is now called Folsom Culture.

Folsom people left more questions for archaeologists than answers. No skeletal remains of a human have ever been found dating from that time in North America. What did they do with their dead? Why have no human bones been found?

Folsom culture left behind only stone implements. Their spear points, chipped from stone, are as mysterious as the people who made them. They are much more finely crafted than necessary. They are, in fact, so skillfully and finely made that they could not be duplicated until very recently, when the techniques used to make them were rediscovered by trial and error. These techniques are called flaking, by which tiny flakes of stone are removed one flake at a time, by either striking the stone with another stone (percussion flaking) or pressing down on it with a piece of antler (pressure flaking). The Folsom spear points somewhat resemble the shape of a laurel leaf, with the edges having been delicately flaked away to a thin sharp cutting edge.

But there is something even more mysterious than their having been made with greater care than necessary. They have parts that they do not need. These unnecessary parts are called flutes, distinct lengthwise grooves on the flat side of the stone. The flutes would have made it slightly easier to mount the spear point on a shaft, but they were not necessary for that. Why the flutes were desirable is a mystery, especially considering the extra amount of time required to do the fluting, which was also done by flaking.

Once Folsom points were discovered and archaeologists learned to look in ten-thousand-year-old layers of strata, Folsom points were soon found in widely scattered sites across North America, especially in the West and Southwest and in Canada. In the 1930s, abundant evidence of an even older culture of Ice Age hunters was discovered when their spear points were uncovered, a culture now called Clovis Culture. Like Folsom Culture, the people of the Clovis Culture also made fluted points, but their points are not as finely crafted and are distinctly different in appearance. Folsom Culture may have evolved from the older Clovis Culture. It also seems apparent that Folsom people had to abandon making their distinctive spear points and develop other kinds of projectile points when large Ice Age mammals became extinct.

With the discoveries of these cultures, the debate over how long humans have been present in North America has been pushed back thousands of years. Some archaeologists have begun digging in strata that are forty thousand and sixty thousand years old, hoping to find something as significant as what George McJunkin found at Dead Horse Gulch.

— D. L. Birchfield

See also:
Clovis Culture.

FOODS AND COOKING, NATIVE AMERICAN

Many of the foods eaten today by people throughout the world were developed by the Native peoples of the Americas or contain ingredients that were produced by the agricultural skills of Native Americans.

Most U.S. schoolchildren have learned about the Native origin of many of the dishes that grace Thanksgiving Day tables to this day. The familiar Thanksgiving foods developed by American Indians include potatoes, corn, green beans, cranberry sauce, sweet potatoes, and pumpkin pie. The turkey itself is a bird native to the Americas. In addition to these items, other foods developed by American Indians that are common not only to holiday dinners but to meals throughout the year include avocados, pineapples, tomatoes, peppers, and squash.

Many food names are also derived from Native words. *Potato*, for example, has its roots in *patata*, a Spanish word derived from *batata*, a term that the first Spaniards to reach the Caribbean heard used by Taino Indians. And *squash* is a shortened form of a term derived from *askootasquash*, a word the early Puritan settlers learned from the Massachuset Indians of present-day New England.

Of all the foods developed by Native American farmers, probably the two that people have come to depend on most for sustenance and livelihood are corn and potatoes. It would be difficult to say which of these two is the greatest single food gift bestowed on the world by Native America, as both are now so widely grown. Corn wins the prize for longevity, however, having been grown in North America for thousands of years before the development of the potato.

Corn, also known as maize, had its beginnings in Mexico about nine thousand years ago with a

This handcrafted figurine is a corn maiden, on display at Isleta Pueblo in New Mexico.

This Navajo man is harvesting corn in Canyon De Chelly on the Navajo Reservation in northeastern Arizona.

At Sutter's Fort in California, a traditional Indian bread is being baked in an Indian adobe oven.

grasslike plant called teosinte. Many years of selecting only the best and largest heads of this grain caused it to evolve into breeds of corn that resemble those that we know today.

As corn approached the size and fullness of the productive food crop presently grown, it began to be passed from tribe to tribe until it reached North America. It arrived in the present-day Southwest about twenty-three hundred years ago, and it reached the East Coast about fifteen hundred years ago. Native peoples in these diverse areas also picked the types of corn that grew best in their climate, giving rise to varieties that grow well in the moist lands of the Southeast, the arid lands of the Southwest, and the short growing season of the North.

The use of the word *corn* to describe this most American of products should not be confused with the word as it is used by people in other parts of the world. In Britain, for example, "corn" refers to any of several cereal plants producing edible seeds, such as wheat, rye, oats, or barley.

For centuries, corn has been a revered plant to many Native peoples. Many tribes have ceremonies or dances celebrating corn, such as the dances of the Pueblo peoples and the Green Corn ceremony of the Creeks and Seminoles, which mark the time when the corn is first getting ripe.

Potatoes, which were native to South America, had not yet reached the tribes of North America at the time the first Europeans arrived. Before the potato arrived on the scene, many North American tribes raised or gathered tubers, the thick or swollen part of various kinds of stems or roots that usually grow underground. One common variety was the tuber of a sunflower. This delicacy may be found today in grocery stores, where it is known as the Sunchoke or Jerusalem artichoke (even though it is not an artichoke and had nothing to do with the city of Jerusalem in its development). Another Native food is the tuber of a plant called *Apios americana,* which is sometimes known as groundnut.

The sweet potato, another edible gift developed by Native farmers, is not a tuber (like the potato) but a root crop closely related to the morning-glory vine. Over thousands of years, the careful selection of sweet potatoes has resulted in the large size and yield of today's varieties.

The pumpkin and its relative, the squash, both of which have decorative as well as culinary uses, have also been raised in North America for thousands of years. Despite the popularity of pumpkins at Halloween, many people do not take full advantage of the delicious and wholesome food properties of this fruit and simply discard the seeds and pulp after turning a pumpkin into a jack-o'-lantern.

Sunflowers are a crop that was also developed by the Indians of North America. Anyone who has seen these incredibly tall plants with thick stems and huge "faces" that follow the sun in unison as it crosses the sky can well imagine the reaction of Europeans who had never seen this "new" plant before. One explorer described it as "a great herb in the form of a Marigold, about six foot [1.8 meters] in height." He reported that the Indians roasted the seeds to eat out of the palms of their hands or ground them into meal for making either bread or broth. Sunflowers have become one of the main oil-bearing plants raised today, and every grocery store carries sunflower oil for cooking. Sunflower seeds are also roasted and sold as a snack food.

Chili peppers were originally grown in parts of North America and have now spread throughout the world. They have long been a staple seasoning in Mexican and Southwest cooking, and they are a key ingredient in the popular and spicy stew that bears the pepper's name—chili. Chilis are also now used in many of the spicy foods of India and China.

Children watch as a Miwok man demonstrates cooking by the use of heated rocks. Clean rocks are heated in a fire, then added to the food being cooked. Native people cooked using this method for many centuries before the introduction of metal pots and other trade items by Europeans.

In North America, the fat and protein provided by animals was balanced by the nutrition that came from corn, squash, beans, and wild plants, all of which were cultivated by Native farmers. At the time of contact between Europeans and Native Americans, beans had been known in Europe and other parts of the world. However, early European explorers found many new types of beans that had been developed by Indians in Mexico and Central America and that had spread north. Today, we know these varieties by many names, including kidney beans, lima beans, navy beans, pinto beans, and string beans.

In addition to the food products yielded by beans and other cultivated plants, most tribes also harvest wild plants for food. Europeans gave many of these plants names that seem strange even today, such as pigweed (*Amaranthus*), duck potato (*Sagittaria*), water lotus (*Nelumbonucifera*), and milkweed (*Asclepias*. Other common foods collected from the wild include blackberries, blueberries, strawberries, raspberries, cranberries, grapes, papaws, acorns, wild rice, and the sap from maple trees to make maple syrup.

Indian cooking is quite varied and differs from one part of North America to another. Differences in climate and region determine how foods will grow in any one area, and foods eaten in one area are often as different from foods in another area as are Chinese and French cooking. For example, the people who live along the seacoasts usually eat fish, oysters, clams, and other products of the sea. The people who live near the Great Lakes in the Northeast and upper Midwest might eat wild rice, venison (deer meat), corn, berries, and foods derived from various wild plants. Today in Oklahoma, wild onion dinners are sponsored by many Native American organizations in the spring.

Most American Indian tribes freely shared their bounty of foods with Europeans. Among many tribes, one of the main teachings is to share food. For the help they gave early European settlers, for their long history of skilled agriculture, for their developing and spreading of edible plants, and for their willingness to share their foods with the rest of the world, American Indians have earned a great deal of credit and gratitude for many of the delicious foods people eat today, not just in North America but all over the world.

— J. Rementer

See also:

Columbian Exchange; Green Corn Ceremony; Native American Contributions.

These thin strips of king salmon are being smoked over an open fire to make salmon jerky, which will last for a long time without refrigeration.

In 1973, during the occupation of Wounded Knee on the Pine Ridge Reservation in South Dakota, a grandson of Chief Red Cloud *(left)* speaks to Sioux medicine man Frank Fools Crow *(center)* and Oglala tribal chairman Richard Wilson *(seated)*.

FOOLS CROW, FRANK (1890–1989)

Born in 1890 on the Pine Ridge Reservation in South Dakota, Frank Fools Crow (Oglala Sioux) was a member of one of the seven campfires of the Lakota Nation. Throughout his life, which lasted for nearly a century, he was a witness to many of the difficult changes and hard times that affected his people, the Lakotas, during the twentieth century. His uncle, the renowned spiritual leader Black Elk, was a vital influence on Fools Crow, who made his life mission the preservation of the ancient traditions and sacred knowledge of his people. He was perhaps one of the best-known and most widely respected medicine men, healing those who were sick and passing on his knowledge to those who wished to learn. He was also the highest-ranking civil chief of all the Lakotas, named ceremonial chief of the Lakota Nation.

Among the Lakota people, a holy man is given the power to heal by Wakan Tanka, the Great Spirit. A medicine man not only holds the ability to heal, but also possesses other unusual powers and abilities, including the ability to see into the future and to receive and interpret messages from the spir-

it world. These types of spiritual leaders, along with traditional customs and ceremonies, are an important facet of Sioux societies. During the late nineteenth and early twentieth centuries, many of these traditions were outlawed by the United States. Many of the ceremonies could be practiced only in secret, and it was spiritual leaders like Frank Fools Crow who were responsible for preserving the old spiritual ways.

Though raised and educated in the traditional ways of his people, Frank Fools Crow was also a product of the larger outside world. At age fourteen, he traveled by train to Salt Lake City to participate in a traditional dancing contest. Later, he competed in other contests, rode in horse races, held employment as a telephone lineman, and toured with a wild west show, traveling as far as Europe in 1921.

As an elder statesman of his tribe, he was sought out by people from miles (kilometers) around for information and advice. He became a public speaker, and in addition to being invited to speak at a wide variety of public events, he made many appearances on radio and television. He made a trip to Washington, D.C., as a representative of

Noted writer, historian, and educator Jack D. Forbes has, through his activism, his scholarship and research, and his teaching, made significant contributions to indigenous American communities.

the Lakota Nation to make a plea to the government for the return of the Black Hills. Called *Paha Sapa*, "the heart of everything that is," the hills are sacred land to the Sioux. When the members of the American Indian Movement (AIM) protested government policies by occupying the town of Wounded Knee, on the Pine Ridge Reservation in South Dakota, in 1973, Frank Fools Crow was part of the delegation seeking to arrive at a peaceful agreement.

Over the course of Frank Fools Crow's life, the Lakota people were faced with an abundance of hardships and trials. They were weakened by such social problems as poverty, substance abuse, and political, military, and cultural oppression. Frank Fools Crow, having preserved the traditional Lakota ways and passing them on, served as a source of strength to his people and to their continuing survival.

SEE ALSO:
American Indian Movement; Black Elk; Black Hills; Wounded Knee (1890); Wounded Knee, Confrontation at (1973).

FORBES, JACK D. (1937–)

Jack D. Forbes, a mixed-blood Powhatan-Lenape born on January 7, 1934, in Long Beach, California, and raised in rural southern California during the Great Depression, is an ethno-historian, writer, and educator. When he was nine years old, his family moved north to Los Angeles, where his keen interest in learning led him to pursue a self-education through reading and studying at the Los Angeles Public Library, the L.A. Southwest Museum, and the L.A. Indian Center. This experience provided the basis for his ongoing interest in the history and perspective of indigenous people. At the University of Southern California, he received his bachelor's degree in social science and philosophy in 1955; his master's degree in history in 1956; and, in 1959, his Ph.D. in history (with concentrations in western North American, Latin American, colonial, and social-intellectual history) and anthropology (with a concentration in North American ethnology).

His lengthy experience as a community activist and his interest in culturally relevant education led Forbes to become one of the founders of D-Q University. As a noted scholar, he has made extensive contributions to historical and cultural research relevant to the indigenous peoples of the Americas. He has also compiled the most thorough research available on mixed-blood Native and African-Americans and is noted for such works on this subject as *Black Africans and Native Americans: Race, Caste, and Color in the Evolution of Red-Black Peoples and Africans* and *Native Americans: The Language of Race and the Evolution of Red-Black People*.

His large body of published work includes 16 books, over 130 scholarly articles, more than a dozen pieces of short fiction, 50 poems in anthologies, and a collection of short stories, *Only Approved Indians*. One of his books, *Columbus and Other Cannibals: The Wetiko Disease of Exploitation, Imperialism and Terrorism*, has been translated into German. *A Guide to the Jack D. Forbes Collection* is available through the Special Collections Department at the University of California in Davis.

Forbes is also the author of "Native Intelligence," a column syndicated in various Native newspapers.

Forbes has been a visiting scholar in England (1981–1982, Warwick; 1986–1987, Oxford; and 1993, Essex) and the Netherlands (1983–1984, Rotterdam). From 1989 to 1994, he was the director of Native American Studies at the University of California, Davis, and from 1994 to 1995, he became chair of that department. Now "semi-retired," he continues to research, write, and provide scholarly presentations and dramatic poetry readings throughout the United States.

SEE ALSO:
D-Q University.

FORT APACHE RESERVATION

The 1,665,000 acres (666,000 hectares) of the Fort Apache Reservation in eastern Arizona are the

Cibecue, a White Mountain Apache town on the Fort Apache Reservation in Arizona.

home of the Coyotero Apaches, which include the Cibecue and White Mountain Apaches. Tribal headquarters are at Whiteriver, Arizona, and today, the Coyoteros are known as the White Mountain Apaches. The reservation consists of a diverse terrain with different ecosystems depending upon the elevation, which is from 2,700 feet to 11,500 feet (819 meters to 3,450 meters).

Fort Apache was founded as a military post in 1863, but in 1922, the U.S. Army decommissioned the post. Fort Apache Reservation adjoins the San Carlos Reservation, and the two were one unit until they were administratively divided in 1897.

Fort Apache has an Indian population of more than 8,500.

A number of tribal economic enterprises offer some employment opportunities. The Fort Apache Timber Company, owned and operated by the White Mountain Apaches, employs about four hundred Apache workers, producing one hundred million board feet (about thirty-seven million meters) of lumber annually, and has a gross annual income of approximately thirty million dollars. Approximately 720,000 acres (288,000 hectares) of the reservation is timberland.

The Fort Apache Recreation Enterprise, begun

Agility and timing are displayed in the calf-roping competition at the White Mountain Apache Rodeo in Arizona.

in 1954, has created much economic activity, including Sunrise ski area and summer resort, three miles (about five kilometers) south of McNary, Arizona. It is open year-round and contributes both jobs and tourist dollars to the local economy. The ski area has seven lifts and generates nine million dollars in revenue per year. Other enterprises owned by the tribe include the White Mountain Apache Motel and Restaurant. The White Mountain Apaches maintain eighteen campgrounds with a total of seven hundred units. The White Mountain Apache Tribal Fair is another important economic event. The unemployment rate on the reservation is about 20 percent.

Some Apache communities, like the Cibecue community, are more conservative and traditional than other Apache communities. The most enduring Apache custom is the girls' puberty ceremony each summer. Clan relatives still play important roles in these ceremonies, when girls become Changing Woman for the four days of their nai'es. These are spectacular public events, which are proudly and vigorously advertised by the tribe. The White Mountain Apaches perform the Sunrise Dance and Mountain Spirit Dance throughout the summer, but their traditional dances are most easily observed at the White Mountain Tribal Fair, which usually occurs on Labor Day weekend at Whiteriver, Arizona.

FORT LARAMIE TREATY OF 1851

The failure of the United States to understand tribal governments meant little hope for lasting agreements when its commissioners and Native leaders met to discuss a treaty in 1851. Steeped in the European tradition of one leader speaking for all, the non-Indian negotiators could not conceive of the layers of Indian government, beginning with the extended families making up the tiospayes (for the Lakota) and leaders given equal powers for different responsibilities—wakiconza, or medicine man, for war, another for negotiations, still another for hunting, for example). Nor did they understand the Indians' consensus form of decisionmaking—where everyone is given time to speak his or her opinion and a position is reached by the group as a whole—and reliance on spiritual guidance.

Numbering more than eight thousand, the Indians—Arapaho, Cheyenne, Lakota, Cros, Assiniboine, Shoshone, Hidatasa, Arikara, and Mandan—finally agreed to come to Horse Creek (later Fort Laramie, in what is now southeast Wyoming) in 1851 for discussions with the U.S. government. Because the meeting was held in their country, the largest group was the Oglala band of the Lakota tribe. Many, like the Crows and Lakotas, were longtime enemies, but no fighting occurred during the meetings.

The Indians came because of their alarm over the increasing flow of non-Indian immigrants, miners, and settlers into and through their country. Indians also faced decimation by smallpox, cholera, and other diseases brought by the whites and the destruction of the buffalo herds the tribes depended upon. The Indians came to Horse Creek with many complaints, while the Euro-Americans came expecting to claim more land for peaceful travel and more army posts.

The treaty worked out at this meeting separated the lands of these tribes into defined areas. Each tribe was assigned to one area, and the United States was given the right to build roads and military posts in Indian territory. In exchange, the government promised to protect the Indians from any crimes by non-Natives and to punish non-Native offenders. The government also agreed to pay $50,000 annually for fifty years, with payments in provisions, merchandise, animals, and agriculture tools. Many of the Indians who had no part in the decision making disagreed with these terms and paid no attention to the agreement. Without discussing it with the Indians, Congress reduced the years for payments to fifteen but actually never provided goods amounting to $50,000 in any year.

In 1994, the Lakotas in their Lakota Summit VII meeting of all Lakota-Dakota-Nakota tribes in the United States and Canada passed a resolution to pursue legislation that would return to them the 1851 treaty lands in the Bighorn Mountains as well as the Black Hills of South Dakota. They limited their claim to the lands currently owned or controlled by the government.

SEE ALSO:
Black Hills; Bozeman Trail and the Battle of a Hundred Slain; Fort Laramie Treaty of 1868.

FORT LARAMIE TREATY OF 1868

In the 1860s, after the United States lost the war on the northern Great Plains for control of the Powder River Territory, which is usually called Red Cloud's War, the U.S. government agreed to close the forts on the Bozeman Trail (in today's eastern Wyoming) and requested treaty negotiations with the Lakotas, Cheyennes, and Arapahos. The war had been fought by the United States in an attempt to keep the Bozeman Trail open; it was a major trail through the present-day states of Montana and Wyoming for immigration from the East to the Oregon country.

The treaty that ended the war, which is known as the 1868 Treaty of Fort Laramie, appeared to be yet another victory for the Lakotas and their allies. In fact, historian Doane Robinson calls Red Cloud's War "the only instance in the history of the United States where the government has gone to war and afterwards negotiated a peace conceding everything demanded by the enemy and exacting nothing in return."

By the terms of this treaty, the U.S. government would abandon the three forts on the Bozeman Trail, close the trail, and provide the Lakotas with rations for thirty years. The United States would pay for lands taken from the Lakotas, Cheyennes, and Arapahos and recognize a large tract of land for the exclusive use of the Lakotas, including the all-important and sacred Black Hills, called *Paha Sapa*, or "the heart of everything that is." The boundaries of this area would be the Missouri River on the east; the Bighorn Mountains on the west; the northern boundary of what is now northern Nebraska on the south; and the forty-sixth parallel on the north. Most important, the treaty reserved to the Lakotas the right to hunt on their unceded lands (lands they had not yielded to the U.S. government) from Nebraska into Montana. The United States would protect this land from non-Native incursions. The treaty also prohibited the United States from building any new roads through these Indian lands. For their part, the Indians would be responsible for handing over any "bad man among the Indians." Only then would U.S. jurisdiction apply.

Congress drew up the treaty and sent a peace commission to Fort Laramie to get Red Cloud's signature. However, even with his terms met, Red Cloud was still hesitant to discuss the treaty. Finally, near the end of October 1868, Red Cloud and one hundred important chiefs went to Fort Laramie. The discussions continued into November, when Red Cloud finally agreed to sign the treaty.

The United States immediately broke the treaty and began waging war against the Indians in their unceded territories. Non-Native Easterners were encouraged to head for the lands that had been reserved to the Indians by the treaty. In direct violation of the treaty, a team of explorers, headed by George Armstrong Custer, publicly documented the presence of gold in the Black Hills. This set off a gold rush into the sacred land of the Black Hills. The United States also never provided the rations and commodities described in the treaty.

Red Cloud quickly realized that he had been tricked. However, having given his word, he never fought against the United States again. He insisted he did not know about some of the terms that non-Natives claimed were included in the treaty, such as giving up Sioux claims to the Nebraska and Kansas territories. The next year, Red Cloud traveled throughout Lakota territory, explaining the true meaning of the treaty to all the chiefs. In 1875, he went to Washington, D.C., to complain to President Ulysses S. Grant. He told the president, "The white children have surrounded me and have left me nothing but an island. . . . I have two mountains in that country [the Black Hills and the Bighorns]. I want the Great Father to make no roads through." President Grant was unsympathetic; in fact, he even removed the soldiers who were supposed to prevent non-Native miners from entering the sacred Black Hills.

For 105 years, the Lakotas and their allies, especially the Cheyennes, sought in vain to have their rights upheld under the Fort Laramie Treaty of 1868. In December 1974, the treaty became part of the trials of several Lakotas and others charged in connection with the seventy-one-day siege at Wounded Knee, which had occurred in 1973 on the Pine Ridge Reservation in South Dakota. Article One of the 1868 Treaty stipulates that Indians will determine when "bad men among them" should be handed over to U.S. authorities. Motions for dismissal of Wounded Knee charges based on Article One were consolidated into the treaty hearing. A successful hearing would dismiss all the charges against the defendants, charges that had been brought by non-Indian grand juries all over South Dakota.

For thirteen days in federal court in Lincoln, Nebraska, Lakota elders, anthropologists, young warriors, Indian and non-Indian historians, and Indian and non-Indian attorneys testified about the Treaty of 1868. All of the witnesses, even the government's witnesses, told the same story: that the United States had unilaterally violated the treaty and that a major part of the treaty that had been violated was Article One, the article that gave Indians jurisdiction over criminal activity by Native people. The United States did not present any evidence to show that it had ever legally taken civil and criminal jurisdiction over the Sioux Nation.

One of the witnesses was Matthew King, who as a child heard Red Cloud talk about the treaty. "The 1868 Treaty is one important thing in Sioux life," King testified. He said the Indians never knew about provisions for the Union Pacific Railroad's use of land and the Indians' loss of mineral rights.

Lakota historian, lawyer, and professor Vine DeLoria, Jr., told the court, "[The Lakota] definitely considered themselves a distinct and separate sovereignty. . . . The United States could not come in and police the people without their consent. . . . [The Lakota] felt that they had beaten the United States and that the United States was suing for peace. To pretend today that the United States was all-powerful during the years when this treaty was being negotiated is simply to read present conditions back into the past and rewrite, falsely, American history."

Judge Warren Urbom ruled against the motion to dismiss. He avoided consideration of issues regarding the treaty by ruling that the questions of sovereignty and jurisdiction were not within the jurisdiction of his court.

"Sometimes the incredible nature of truth makes falsehood acceptable, and thus it was in this case," DeLoria reacted.

Urbom did have an emotional reaction to the testimony and included it in his decision. "It is an ugly history. White Americans may retch at the recollection of it."

DeLoria said Urbom's ruling stemmed from the political nature of the trial—". . . that the Sioux might be a quasi-independent nation inside the United States—was simply inconceivable and unacceptable to the administration in power and the society which it represented," he said.

A number of Indian organizations, Native and non-Native lawyers, the International Indian Treaty Organization at the United Nations, and coalitions of people across the United States continue to work for treaty rights for all Indian people, including the Native people who are parties to the 1868 Treaty of Fort Laramie.

— C. Hamilton

SEE ALSO:

Black Hills; Bozeman Trail and the Battle of a Hundred Slain; Custer, George Armstrong; Federal Land; Fort Laramie Treaty of 1851; Red Cloud; Wounded Knee, Confrontation at (1973).

FORTY-NINE DANCES

A night of social dancing now known as a "49" originated among the Kiowa people from Oklahoma many years ago, before the Department of the Interior, Office of Indian Affairs, tried to put an end to Kiowa ceremonial dances in the early 1890s. These dances, which are now used for social dancing, are sometimes still referred to as war journey dances and war journey songs because their original use was for singing and dancing to honor Kiowa warriors prior to venturing out on war exhibitions. The men sang the songs while the women accompanied them in the background. Both men and women participated in the dances.

Usually, the warriors and their companions would get together outside in the early evenings before going off to hunt or to do battle. Evenings were spent singing songs that were pleasing to many couples. There were favorite songs and new compositions sung throughout the night. They danced in nontraditional outfits, wearing everyday clothes.

Since the early days of war journey dances, times have changed, and so have the songs and dancers. Today, most dances occur during the summertime because of the weather. The dance is usually held outside in an open field or area where many people can congregate and socialize during the event.

The dance starts when the singers come together holding a drum. The major clue to anyone close enough to hear the beating of the drum is the first song, called the "starting song." The singers start beating the drum with their drumsticks in frequent rhythms called a drumroll. This rolling of the drum signifies to the people that the dance is starting. Everybody then starts to gather around the singers forming a circle, sometimes locking their arms together.

Dance steps are not fancy, but simple, slow, and smooth side steps to the left as they face forward, circling clockwise around the singers all at the same time. At larger 49 dances, it is not unusual to see dancers form circles of three-to-five rings deep surrounding the singers. The men singers sing a long series of war journey songs before taking a break. The songs and dances continue on throughout the night with no set time to conclude the dance. The women support the men singers by accompanying their voices well into the first part of each song. If words are included in the songs, they usually are expressing their feelings of love toward their companions. The dance continues with the series of songs, while taking breaks at various intervals.

Today, war journey dances have taken on a different dimension toward more intertribalism. Rather than building enthusiasm for war as in earlier times, the dance is performed for both the fun and the cultural significance it affords.

SEE ALSO:
Forty-nine Songs; Kiowa.

FORTY-NINE SONGS

Songs for a night of social dancing known as a "49" originated as war journey songs of the Kiowas. The term *49* has numerous interpretations, but the most prominent refers to the glory days of the Kiowas around 1849. One intent of the songs was to make couples feel good while courting one another. Some of the songs are serious, while others are often humorous, and still others take on the ups and downs of personal relationships. Some older Kiowas still refer to them as courting dances and courting songs.

War journey songs and dances have become very popular with younger Indian people for social dancing at a 49, which is usually held during the outdoor summer months. For a 49, singers usually come together after a large powwow or Indian gathering and seek out a large area where dancers can congregate in a large circular formation. About four to ten men hold the drum up from the ground while facing forward toward the drum in a tight circle. Men start the songs, while the women singers accompany them, singing in harmony. The instruments that they use consist of a large cowhide drum, drumsticks, and their natural voices.

The first war journey song is a calling song. The song starts by having the singers beat the drum all together very hard at the beginning. The rolling of the drum signifies the calling of the dancers. At a much later time, the singers lead into the song.

Usually, the more accomplished singers take the lead by starting the songs. Depending on the song's popularity, 49 songs are normally repeated four times. The drumming rhythm is a constantly alternating soft and hard pattern, while the men's voices are at their peak volume. Accomplished singers have great stamina and the ability to pound steady beats on the drum and sing for hours at a time. Once a song is started, the other singers support by singing and drumming together throughout the entire song and a series of songs until they get tired. Then, the singers take a short break and start back up again.

This format continues throughout the summer nights across the country. Among the favorite selections of war journey songs is one called the "One-eyed Ford."

When the dance is over sweetheart,
I will take you home in my one-eyed Ford,
hay ya eye ho eye ho eye ho eye ya.

Many Kiowa war journey songs were originally composed with Kiowa words. Today, many English words can be heard in the songs as a result of intertribalism—a mixing and sharing of Native cultures. More popular 49 singers can have a repertoire of one hundred songs or more, all sung from memory. These 49 singers are usually accomplished singers with a personal knowledge of many other intertribal songs.

With so many different Indian songs and dances coming together in all parts of the country, Indian people have distinguished differences in song and dance styles by calling them either "Northern" or "Southern." Forty-nine songs, therefore, have a Southern Plains' affiliation, having originated among the Kiowa people from Oklahoma.

In Oklahoma, many large social powwows have included war journey songs within their social dance portion, which also includes the round dance, two-step, snake dance, and rabbit dance. The popular round dances, Oklahoma two-step, and the 49 social dance songs are becoming a part of modern intertribal powwow lifestyle throughout the continent.

SEE ALSO:
Forty-nine Dances; Kiowa.

FOX

SEE Sac and Fox.

FRANCE

Contact between the European power of France and Native Americans began with the explorer Jacques Cartier in 1534. Cartier found two Iroquois fishing in the Bay of Chaleur that summer and promptly kidnapped them. In 1535, the following year, the king of France, Francois I, supported Cartier's further explorations in the so-called New World. Cartier made his way up the St. Lawrence River to Mohawk settlements in what is now Quebec and to Wyandot (Huron) and Onondaga settlements where Montreal is now located. While there, he was asked to help heal the sick. This established the beginning of generally friendly relations between the French and the Indians. From the viewpoint of historian Francis Parkman, "Spanish civilization crushed the Indian; English civilization scorned and neglected him; French civilization embraced and cherished him."

In 1536, during Cartier's second visit, he kidnapped the Chief Donnacona, his two sons, and eight of his band and took them back to France. They all died in France, after being baptized, before

A depiction of Jacques Cartier's first visit to Hochelaga in 1535. Cartier was the first European to explore the Gulf of St. Lawrence and the St. Lawrence River.

Cartier could return to the St. Lawrence in 1541. In 1540, the king made the conversion of the Indians to Christianity an official goal of the French colonial effort. During Cartier's third voyage, in 1541, he established a small colony at Cap Rouge. On this trip, he left two young French boys with the Indians in exchange for the two Indian children he had taken in 1536.

French exploration then basically stopped for about fifty years. However, these early exchanges between the French and the Native peoples of the St. Lawrence area served the French well. The Natives of the area were of the Algonquian language family, the largest language family in North America. Algonquian languages extended all the way to the Blackfeet in the Rocky Mountains and also included the Wyandots. This common linguistic ground helped the French later during the expansion of the fur trade and in their missionary efforts among the tribes.

In 1600, a trading post was set up at the mouth of the Saguenay River, and in 1602, the Company of New France obtained a royal charter to the fur trade from Florida to the Arctic Circle. In return for this charter, the company promised to settle four thousand colonists in New France within fifteen years. This company and the ones that followed never did well settling colonists; they did excel, however, in learning from and using the Indians for the fur trade and for fighting their European rivals, who outnumbered the French.

The French adopted the Indian canoe. This helped the French explorers, known as *voyageurs*, explore the entire Great Lakes chain and most of the rivers that fed into them, all the way to their headwaters. In addition, the French explored the entire Mississippi, Missouri, and Arkansas Rivers. In the southeastern region of the North American continent, they allied themselves with the Choctaws after founding the colony of Louisiana at the mouth of the Mississippi River in 1700. Also, many of the French intermarried with Indians and adopted Indian ways and languages. This gave them great advantages in forging alliances with Indians in matters of trade, missionary efforts, and war. By 1640, more than one thousand baptisms had taken place in North America. The first missions were established in the north during 1632–1633, and Jesuit missionaries were soon making dictionaries of the Indian languages throughout the French-explored areas of North America.

Despite their first friendships with the Hurons, the French found themselves at war with the five tribes that formed the Iroquois Confederacy. The Iroquois were eventually forced to become allied with the British and continued to alternately war with and make peace with the French and their Indian allies. During the French and Indian War, 1754–1763, the British suffered a major defeat at Fort Duquesne (now Pittsburgh, Pennsylvania). One of the survivors was a young colonial officer, George Washington. Washington himself declared that Indian allies were worth twice as much as Euro-American troops. In the Southeast, the French and their Choctaw allies also fought against the English and their reluctant allies, the Cherokees and Chickasaws.

The final French defeat and surrender occurred in 1760 at Montreal, Quebec. This shifted the balance of power from Native nations that had allied themselves with colonial powers to Britain, now the major colonial power in North America. Even in defeat, the French governor of New France attempted to look out for the Native allies of the French by including a section for their welfare in the treaty signed at the surrender of Montreal. Because of this, the British attempted to establish a large reserve for them between the Ohio and Mississippi Rivers. The French fur trade, now taken over by the British, continued. It was still run by French Canadians and mixed-blood Métis traders and voyagers. Their working language remained French. At the end of the French and Indian War, most of North America became British. The "French Indians" exchanged their French peace medals for English ones on King George's birthday in 1764.

In 1803, the U.S. government completed the Louisiana Purchase. This single sale included almost the entire Great Plains between the Mississippi River and the Rocky Mountains. It doubled the size of the United States. With this completed, the French control of and influence over the Indians of North America began to diminish.

In Canada, the Métis traders were later responsible for creating the Métis Nation in the west. They fought against the English settlers in 1869–1870 and 1885. The Métis leader during this fight was Louis Riel, who is now recognized in Canada as a national hero. Riel fought to preserve the old trading way of life, with its Indian, French, and Catholic values. Today, Canada's principal French-speaking population resides in the province of Quebec, where Native people (many now prefer to be called First Nations people) are negotiating with the Quebec and Canadian governments to cancel a number of large hydroelectric dam projects that would flood much of their reserve lands.

— J. D. Berry

SEE ALSO:

Canada, Native–Non-Native Relations in; French and Indian War; Iroquois Confederacy; James Bay Hydro-Electric Project; Louisiana Purchase; Métis; Wyandot (Huron).

SUGGESTED READINGS:

Debo, Angie. *A History of the Indians of the United States*. Norman: University of Oklahoma Press, 1970.

Dickason, Olive Patricia. *Canada's First Nations: A History of Founding Peoples from Earliest Times*. Norman: University of Oklahoma Press, 1992.

Eccles, W. J. *The Canadian Frontier, 1534–1760*. Toronto: Holt, Rinehart and Winston, 1969.

Trigger, Bruce G. *The Indian and the Heroic Age of New France*. Ottawa: Canadian Historical Association, 1970.

FRANKLIN, BENJAMIN (1706–1790)

Benjamin Franklin's life frequently involved the lives, societies, and affairs of Native Americans. As a printer, he published accounts of Indian treaties for more than two decades. Franklin began his diplomatic career by representing the colony of Pennsylvania at councils with the Iroquois and their allies. His designs for the Albany Plan of Union and later Articles of Confederation contain elements of the Native American systems of confederation that he had come to know as a diplomat. Franklin also speculated in Native land.

Franklin first read the Iroquois's urgings to unite when he was a printer of Indian treaties. By the early 1750s, Franklin was more directly involved in diplomacy itself; at the same time, he became an early forceful advocate of colonial union. All of these circumstantial strings were tied together in the summer of 1754, when colonial representatives, Franklin among them, met with Iroquois sachems (leaders) at Albany to address issues of mutual concern and to develop the Albany Plan of Union. Its design echoes both English and Iroquois precedents, and it would become a rough draft for the Articles of Confederation a generation later.

Even before the Albany Conference in 1754, Franklin had used Iroquois examples of unity as he sought to shame the reluctant colonists into some form of union. In 1751, in order to drive home a point, he engaged in a racial slur (while, in fact, Franklin had a healthy respect for the Iroquois): "It would be a strange thing . . . if Six Nations of Ignorant savages should be capable of forming such an union and be able to execute it in such a manner that it has subsisted for ages and appears indissoluble, and yet that a like union should be impractical for ten or a dozen English colonies, to whom it is more necessary and must be more advantageous, and who cannot be supposed to want an equal understanding of their interest."

In October of 1753, Franklin attended a treaty council at Carlisle, Pennsylvania. At this council with the Iroquois and Ohio Indians (Twightees, Delawares, Shawnees, and Wyandots), Franklin absorbed the rich imagery and ideas of the Six Nations at close range. On October 1, 1753, he watched the Oneida chief, Scarrooyady, and a Mohawk, Cayanguileguoa, express sympathy to the Ohio Indians for their losses against the French. Franklin listened while Scarrooyady recounted the origins of the Great Law to the Ohio Indians.

Franklin used his image of Indians and their societies as a critique of Europe: "The Care and Labour of providing for Artificial and fashionable Wants, the sight of so many Rich wallowing in superfluous plenty, while so many are kept poor and distress'd for want; the Insolence of Office . . . [and] restraints of Custom, all contrive to disgust them [Indians] with what we call civil Society."

Franklin described the Indians' passion for liberty while making it a patriotic rallying cry. Openly admiring Indians' notions of happiness while seeking a definition that would suit the new nation, Franklin wrote: "All the Indians of North America not under the dominion of the Spaniards are in that natural state, being restrained by no Laws, having no Courts, or Ministers of Justice, no Suits, no prisons, no prisons, no governors vested with any Legal Authority. The persuasion of Men distinguished by Reputation of Wisdom is the only Means by which others are govern'd, or rather led—and the State of the Indians was probably the first State of all Nations."

— B. E. Johansen

SEE ALSO:

Albany Plan of Union; American Revolution; Constitution, United States; Iroquois Confederacy; Jefferson, Thomas.

SUGGESTED READINGS:

Aldridge, Alfred O. *Benjamin Franklin: Philosopher and Man.* Philadelphia: J. B. Lippincott, 1965.

Franklin, Benjamin. *The Autobiography of Benjamin Franklin,* ed. John Bigelow. Philadelphia: J. B. Lippincott, 1868.

Grinde, Donald A., Jr., and Bruce E. Johansen. *Exemplar of Liberty: Native America and the Evolution of Democracy.* Los Angeles: University of California, 1991.

FREEDMEN

Some tribal members of the Cherokee, Chickasaw, Choctaw, Creek, and Seminole Nations owned slaves from colonial times throughout the Civil War period. Slaveholding among these Southern tribes was mostly in mixed-blood families by white men who had joined the tribe by marrying an Indian woman or by the mixed-blood children of such marriages. Though only a few people in each tribe owned slaves, some of them owned large numbers. Robert Jones, a mixed-blood Choctaw, owned more than five hundred African-American slaves and operated a large plantation with slave labor.

During the Indian removal period of the 1830s, many of the slaveholding Indians took their slaves with them to Indian Territory, now known as Oklahoma. When the Civil War started, the United States removed its troops from Indian Territory, leaving the Indian nations defenseless against the forces of the Confederacy. Such removal of federal troops was a violation of treaties, in which the

An 1866 woodcut of a Freedmen's Bureau in Tennessee. In Indian Territory, the Five Civilized Tribes adopted their freedmen as tribal citizens after the Civil War, though it required a generation of political maneuvering on the part of the United States.

United States had obligated itself to protect the Indian nations of the territory. Left without federal protection, some members of some tribes fought with the Confederates and some fought with the Union. Once the Emancipation Proclamation had been signed by President Abraham Lincoln and the Civil War was over, the slaveholding Indians had to free their slaves. These former slaves were called freedmen.

Because some of the tribes had entered into diplomatic relations with the Confederacy, the U.S. government demanded that the tribes negotiate new treaties with the United States. At a council meeting held at Fort Smith, Arkansas, the tribes were chastised for their participation with the South, despite the fact that many tribal members fought with the North.

In the new treaties, the federal government, for the most part, was interested in securing a right-of-way for railroads through the Indian nations, but it also forced the tribes to provide provisions for their freedmen. Of those slaveholding nations, the Cherokees had already emancipated their slaves during the war.

In October of 1865, Brevet Major General John B. Sanborn of the United States Volunteers started his new assignment to regulate freedmen and Indian relations in the Indian Territory. General Sanborn released his first directive through a series of circulars on January 1, 1866. He ordered Indian agents to explain to the tribes the new relation between them and their former slaves. Agents were to explain to the freedmen that they were now free and no longer held by slavery. They were to ensure that contracts were made for wages and to sign poor freedmen up for rations with their respective tribes.

General Sanborn wanted each head of household of the freedmen to be issued 160 acres (64 hectares) and for land to be provided for their children. He authorized the freedmen to remain in the Indian nations and to cultivate the lands they occupied and directed the army to protect any freedmen from harm. Sanborn left his office on April 30, 1866, and was replaced by Elijah Sells, the superintendent of Indian Affairs for the Southern Superintendency.

The Creeks, Seminoles, and Cherokees adopted some of the freedmen. These adoptions provided for the freedmen the rights of a tribal citizen of that nation, which included the use of tribal land and provisions for losses sustained from the war.

The Cherokees, as well as the other tribes, were divided about the provisions for their former slaves and established a time limit that freedmen had to meet to become citizens. Those who did not return from the war or other places by the time limit were later rejected as citizens. The Chickasaws and Choctaws resisted giving citizenship and rights to their freedmen, relying instead on the provisions of their new treaty with the United States, which obligated the United States to remove the freedmen from the Choctaw Nation if the Choctaws did not confer citizenship on them. The United States ignored those provisions and continued to pressure the Choctaws and Chickasaws into adopting the freedmen as tribal citizens, which they finally did, but not until near the end of the century.

Despite the disagreement among the tribes concerning the citizenship and rights of the freedmen, many of the freedmen made contributions to the tribes as interpreters and politicians.

— S. Arkeketa

SEE ALSO:
Civil War, U.S., Indians in the; Five Civilized Tribes; Oklahoma; Removal Act, Indian.

FRENCH AND INDIAN WAR

Between 1689 and 1763, England and France fought four wars. Each of the European conflicts had its counterpart in North America, although each of the wars was known by a different name there: The War of the League of Augsburg (1689–1697) was known in North America as King William's War, the War of Spanish Succession (1701–1713) as Queen Anne's War, the War of Austrian Succession (1744–1748) as King George's War, and the Seven Years' War (1756–1763) as the French and Indian War. The first three wars were indecisive, but the last war greatly changed the political structure of North America.

In terms of American Indian history, the French and Indian War is significant because at just the time when Indians might have been joining together, they instead were divided in their support for

A depiction of General Edward Braddock's English army being attacked in the woods of Pennsylvania by French forces and their Indian allies in July 1755 during the French and Indian War.

the English and French and fought one another. The events that led to the French and Indian War began in 1752. The French realized that if they were to limit English expansion west, they must control the Ohio Valley. If the English moved into the Ohio region, a wedge would be driven between French holdings in Canada and Louisiana.

In June of 1752, the French trader Charles Langlade led a force of 150 Ottawa and Ojibwe (Chippewa) warriors against the main British trading post at Pickawillany. Pickawillany was the home of the Miami chief known as Old Britain and home to 50 British traders. In the attack, Old Britain and 13 other Miamis and 4 English traders were killed.

Following up this success, the new governor of Canada, the Marquis Duquesne, sent a force of fifteen hundred men down the St. Lawrence and into the Great Lakes region and built forts at Presq' Isle and Le Boeuf. Impressed by the large French force and by the forts, the Miamis, Sauks, Potawatomies, Ojibwes, Lenapes (Delawares), Shawnees, and the Great Lakes–area Iroquois all joined with the French.

On December 11, 1753, Major George Washington approached the commander of the fort at Le Boeuf and presented him with a note from the governor of Virginia telling him that the French were in the area illegally and ordered them to leave. The French refused to go, and Washington returned in 1754 with a force to drive them out. He then engaged the French in a small skirmish near Great Meadows in Pennsylvania. The French lost the skirmish, and one Frenchman was killed. Washington then built a small fort, Fort Necessity, near Great Meadows but was forced to surrender to a superior French force on July 4, 1754. Washington and his men were allowed to return to Virginia. At about this same time, the French also took over the English trading post at present-day Pittsburgh and built a fort called Fort Duquesne.

The American British colonies were very concerned about these moves by the French. They met at the Albany Congress and agreed to fight together against the French, and they appealed to King George II for help. The New England colonies and the colonies of New York, Pennsylvania, and Maryland were also very concerned that the Iroquois Confederacy might join the French.

The English had one man who would play a large role in maintaining Iroquois support for the English—William Johnson. This nephew of Sir Peter Warren came to America to oversee his uncle's landholdings. Soon after he arrived, he became fascinated by the Iroquois he met. He learned the Mohawk language and married the daughter of Iroquois leader Joseph Brant (Thayendanegea). Johnson also became a close friend to the famous Iroquois chief, Hendrick. Hendrick agreed to support the British against the French.

The British Crown responded to the colonists' plea by sending Major General Edward Braddock and two five-hundred-man regiments. The British also supplied the colonials with plans for a four-pronged attack to push the French back into Canada. With his two regiments and two hundred Virginia militia, General Braddock would attack Fort Duquesne. William Shirley, the British colonial administrator who served as governor of Massachusetts, would lead two regiments of Massachusetts militia against Fort Niagara. William Johnson would lead New York and New Jersey militias and Iroquois allies against the fort at Crown Point. Finally, a British force under Lieutenant Colonel Monckton would attack Fort Beausejour at the head of the Bay of Fundy in Canada.

Many people have learned a faulty version of the history of the battle that is called "Braddock's Defeat." The myth that exists around this battle represents Edward Braddock as a foolish and vain general who refused to listen to advice from George Washington and blundered into an ambush. He then refused to let his men move into the trees to fight "Indian style." But like many myths, the myth of Braddock's Defeat is almost completely false. As he moved on Fort Duquesne, Braddock expected to be ambushed, and he crossed and recrossed the Monongahela River to avoid likely ambush sites. He also placed an advance force of two hundred men ahead of the main force, under the command of Lieutenant Colonel Thomas Gage, so that the main body of his force could be protected from a surprise attack.

On the morning of July 9, 1755, Gage's advance guard made contact with a French force made up of 108 French regulars, 146 Canadian militia members, and 637 Indians. The men formed up and started to deliver volleys of musket fire. The Canadian militia fled at the first British volley, and the French commander was killed by the third volley. Gage brought up and employed his cannon, and the Indians started to fall back. The French regulars advanced, however, and held the center of the French line. The Indians then flanked Gage's men on both sides and began to shoot into the massed British troops. The advance guard fell back into the main body of the British army, causing great confusion, and the Indians continued to flank and shoot into the milling British troops. The Indians stayed in the trees; one British survivor of the battle said that none of the British troops ever saw more than six Indians at one time, and many of the British never saw even one Indian.

Braddock's Defeat was unlike other battles in the French and Indian War in that Indian warriors played an essential role in the victory. In the other battles of the war, Indian warriors played a supporting role or no role at all.

The first element of the British plan had failed, and other parts of the four-pronged attack were also unsuccessful. Shirley didn't launch an attack because the French had gained the total British battle plan in captured papers from the Braddock battlefield and were too well prepared for his action against Fort Niagara. Johnson had some minor successes but couldn't get his troops to attack Crown Point. The only commander who achieved victory was Monckton, who took Fort Beausejour.

In the summer of 1756, the English and French officially declared war on one another, and the conflict was waged in Europe, Africa, India, North America, and on islands all around the world. As the war continued in North America, the initial victories continued to go to the French. The French first took Fort Oswego. Impressed by this victory, more Indian tribes went over to the French side. In August of 1757, the French took Fort William Henry.

In 1758, a large British army arrived in North America, and the tide began to turn. Lord Jeffrey Amherst took the French fort at Louisbourg, as General John Forbes took Fort Duquesne. William Johnson and his army took Fort Niagara. The only French success in 1758 was a French repulse of an attack on Fort Ticonderoga.

The final, and most decisive battle of the war, was fought on September 12, 1759. In a daring attack, Major General James Wolfe and his men scaled the cliffs leading to the Plains of Abraham surrounding Quebec City and assembled before the town. The French commander, Louis Joseph, Marquis de Montcalm, accepted the challenge and marched his troops out to do battle. But Montcalm's troops proved no match for the perfect volleys delivered by Wolfe's well-disciplined regiments. Even though both generals died on the field of battle, the victory went to the British. In 1760, Montreal fell, and the French had lost the war in North America.

The war ended officially in 1763 with the Treaty of Paris, and the British gained Canada. The Indians had lost an ally in the French and prepared themselves to face the English expansion into their territories.

— T. Colonnese

SEE ALSO:

American Revolution; Canada, Native–Non-Native Relations in; England; France; Iroquois Confederacy.

FUR TRADE

SEE American Fur Company, the; Beavers; France.

GAIWIIO

SEE Handsome Lake.

GALL (1840–1894)

Hunkpapa Sioux leader Gall, who was also known as Pizi, helped fight for the control of the Bozeman Trail and the sacred Black Hills of South Dakota, which are called *Paha Sapa* by the Sioux. During his remarkable life, Gall witnessed some of the late nineteenth century's most extraordinary and controversial events on the northern Great Plains. He maintained close ties with the greatest Indian leaders of the northern Plains, and he dined in stately rooms with important government officials and members of Congress. Amid such notable events, Gall is perhaps most widely known as one of the famed war chiefs responsible for the fall of Lieutenant Colonel George Armstrong Custer and some two hundred soldiers of the Seventh Cavalry in the 1876 Battle of the Little Bighorn.

At the time of the Battle of the Little Bighorn, Gall was a thirty-six-year-old adopted brother of Sitting Bull. Gall had grown up in the Hunkpapa camp as an orphan and later became Sitting Bull's lieutenant, a war chief of the tribe. Gall distinguished himself as a warrior early in life. During the many skirmishes over control of the Bozeman Trail in 1866 and 1867, Gall devised shrewd military tactics that he later used in the struggles for control of the Black Hills. During the ongoing battles over the Black Hills, Gall was Sitting Bull's principal military advisor.

But it was Gall's keen military planning in the defeat of Custer at the Little Big Horn that earned him his greatest reputation among the Hunkpapa Sioux as a war chief and principal military strategist. Gall is credited with leading his Hunkpapa warriors to force back Major Reno's column away from a Hunkpapa village and chasing them across the river and into the bluffs. He then, alongside Crazy Horse, led his warriors into a fight against Custer's column. As a fierce protector of his people, Gall was responsible for the successful tactics that led to Custer's ultimate defeat. He later made the statement, "If you had a country which was very valuable, which had always belonged to your people . . . and men of another race came to take it away by force, what would your people do? Would they fight?"

Following the Battle of the Little Bighorn, Gall journeyed to Canada with Sitting Bull and many other Hunkpapa followers. In 1881, he returned to the United States along with three hundred of his people and surrendered at Fort Buford. Gall was then relocated to the Standing Rock Sioux Reservation in North Dakota, where he established friendly relations with an Indian agent named James McLaughlin. Gall later himself became a reservation agent and was characterized as being an ideal agency chief, becoming a negotiator for treaties that divided the Sioux lands into their pre-

Chief Gall of the Hunkpapa Sioux was one of the Indian leaders who met the attack of Lieutenant Colonel George Armstrong Custer's Seventh U.S. Cavalry on an Indian village in 1876 in present-day southeastern Montana and defeated Custer and his troops at Little Bighorn Creek.

sent-day arrangement. However, Gall's partnership and peacekeeping relations with the government was not well received by other Indians, including those who had been his military allies in previous years.

SEE ALSO:
Black Hills; Bozeman Trail and the Battle of a Hundred Slain; Crazy Horse; Custer, George Armstrong; Little Bighorn, Battle of the; Siouan Nations; Sitting Bull.

GAMES

The North American continent at the time of European contact was a continent at play. So many different kinds of games were being played, under so many different regional and tribal variations and under different names, that scholars who have attempted to survey the reports of early observers have uncovered an almost unmanageable and bewil-

dering amount of material. Broadly speaking, the games can be organized into two categories: games of skill and games of chance.

Of the games of skill, which were also frequently athletic competitions, none was more important than the one that is today most commonly called stickball. The modern collegiate sport of lacrosse is derived from it. But as played in earlier times, its modern descendant seems tame.

Stickball was called *ishtaboli* by the Choctaws, who had a passion for it that amazed European and American observers. The game was played with slight variations in different regions of the continent. American artist George Catlin painted scenes of stickball competitions of the Choctaws in the valleys of the Ouachita Mountains of present-day southeastern Oklahoma and of the Sioux on the Great Plains.

There were some differences in the way these two nations played the game. The Choctaws favored the use of two sticks for each player, called *kapucha* sticks, one for each hand. The Sioux only

In this undated painting, Sioux ballplayers vigorously participate in a game of stickball. The modern college sport of lacrosse is derived from the game, which was important to Indians throughout the continent.

Site of an ancient pre-Columbian Taino ballpark in Puerto Rico. Indigenous games played with balls are common to virtually every tribe in the Western Hemisphere.

used one stick per player. There were minor variations in the way scores were tallied and in the dimensions of the playing surface. But on the whole, the game was largely the same throughout the eastern half of the continent.

Both men and women had stickball teams. Often the men would play a match, followed by a match by the women. Among the Choctaws, teams usually consisted of people from the same town, who might play the team of a neighboring town, from the other side of the nation, or even a team from a neighboring tribe. Occasionally, disputes between tribes might be settled on the outcome of a game of ball. In one reported instance, the Choctaws and the Creeks were said to have determined a territorial claim to a watershed between them on the outcome of such a game, which the Creeks were said to have won by a narrow margin.

The ball for these games was about the size of a modern tennis ball, usually made of hair stuffed inside a rawhide cover. The sticks, made of slender pieces of hickory and about thirty inches (seventy-six centimeters) long, had a webbed pocket at the end. The ball was controlled by catching it in the pocket, after which a player might attempt to advance it by running and carrying the ball inside the pocket or by hurling it to a distant teammate, who might try to catch it on the fly or on the bounce, depending upon how closely he was being guarded by opposing players. The ball might be pitched to a trailing teammate, and then the lead player might try to run interference for the ball carrier.

There were no rules. The progress of the ball toward one goal or the other could be aided or impeded by whatever means a player might find desirable. Tackling and even violent collisions were common, and so were broken bones. Occasionally, there were even deaths. Injury and death during a game was viewed as a natural part of the competition and carried no penalties.

The playing field was ordinarily large, several hundred yards long, and there were often several

These Native youngsters are engaged in a game of sandlot football on the Tohono O'odham Reservation in Arizona. Some Indian players, such as Olympic champion Jim Thorpe, achieved greatness in the game of football. Thorpe also served as the first president of the National Football League (NFL).

hundred players on each team. The object of the game was to move the ball down the field and hurl it against an upright post, which counted one point. Games were long and grueling; frequently a score of one hundred points would be required to win.

Since they required great stamina, the games were considered to be an excellent preparation for the rigors of warfare. For this reason—and because of their intensity—the game was frequently referred to as "the brother of war."

The game never failed to excite a sense of awe in early observers, and the behavior of spectators drew almost as much attention as the game itself. Hundreds of spectators screamed with glee or disdain at every turn of fortune on the field of play, as though a thing of great importance hung in the balance. Usually it did, and usually that thing consisted of virtually all of the movable possessions of the people of the town. They wagered everything on the outcome. With so much at stake, not only was the game itself conducted and cheered with great passion, but preparations for the game were

carried out with exacting care. Honored elderly men who had spent their whole lives learning medicine would sit up all night long before a game, near the goalpost of their team, solemnly smoking tobacco and contemplating thoughts that might help their team to win.

Though the game itself was played with great exertion, and physical contact was violent and injuries frequent, contestants almost never engaged in violence off the field. Instances in which a game did result in off-field violence were so rare that they became matters of deep concern for tribal leaders. In one reported instance, a game between Choctaws and Creeks erupted in violence when an angry player grabbed a weapon and attacked an opposing player. Other players got their weapons, and before elders could intervene, dozens of the best ballplayers of each nation lay dead. Such a rare occurrence shocked both nations.

At least one attempt was made to show exhibitions of stickball games in American cities. In the late 1820s, Dr. Gideon Lincecum, who lived on the edge of the Choctaw country in Mississippi and had learned fluent Choctaw, organized a traveling exhibition consisting of about forty players. In his autobiography, written late in life, he recalled the tour as having been well received, though it barely brought in enough money to pay its expenses.

Today, stickball is still played by communities of American Indians. Though it lacks the degree of violence of earlier days, it is played with no less exertion and enthusiasm. In July of each year, hosted by the Mississippi Band of Choctaw Indians near Philadelphia, Mississippi, the best teams gather during the Choctaw Fair for the World Championship Stickball Competition.

Many other games of skill were played using balls of different varieties. Perhaps the most widespread game required rolling a smooth rounded stone a good distance and then, while the stone was still rolling, hurling a javelinlike spear ahead of the stone in an attempt to predict, by where the spear landed, the precise spot where the stone would stop.

Many skilled athletic games involved long-distance running. These competitions were so widespread as to be virtually universal. Their popularity is especially high among nations of the Southwest. Today, long-distance running is still a feature of many celebrations of Native peoples throughout that region, including the Pueblos and Apaches.

Feathered dart games were also widespread, with the darts being made of everything from slender reeds to corncobs. Often the darts were thrown at net hoops. Many different games involved the use of different kinds of hoops, and some incorporated poles and sticks. In some games, a hoop was propelled by a stick toward an intended object; in other games, poles were hurled through a moving hoop. Specially feathered arrows, rings, stones, disks, counting sticks, and carved objects were all used in one kind of game or another.

Games of chance can be divided into dice games and guessing games. Dice games are played in silence, but guessing games are accompanied by singing and drumming.

Young Slavey Indians (Dene) participating in a snowshoe race at a spring festival at Trout Lake in the Northwest Territories, Canada.

An indigenous American Indian four-stick game of the Klamath people of southwest Oregon.

continent and is still actively played today in Indian centers in urban areas and on reservations. Often a team game, it can be a social event as well as a game. The game can be played entirely by gesture, which made it easy for intertribal play. Records of its use have been found for dozens of tribes speaking many different languages. It involves the passing of objects from hand to hand, from person to person, one a marked object and one unmarked. The player tries to pick the unmarked one.

The wide variety of games in the Americas, both games of skill and games of chance, have been found to have developed here. There is no indication that any of them have been imported to the continent.

— D. L. Birchfield

SUGGESTED READINGS:

Culin, Stewart. *Games of the North American Indians*, Bureau of American Ethnology Annual Report 24. Washington, D.C.: Smithsonian Institution, 1902–1903.

Swanton, John R. *The Indians of the Southeastern United States*, Bureau of American Ethnology Bulletin 137. Washington, D.C.: Smithsonian Institution, 1946.

Many different games involved the use of various kinds of dice. The dice might be carved from wood or bone or fashioned from stone; they might be seeds that had been painted different colors on each side or made from nearly an endless variety of other materials. One common dice game used a bowl with six or eight dice in it. Each player tapped the bottom of the bowl hard enough to cause the dice to jump and rearrange the values they displayed. Variations of the same sort of game were played simply by casting the dice upon a blanket or skin.

Specially carved gambling sticks were widely used in guessing games. Sets of these might include fifty or sixty pieces of finely carved wooden cylinders, with markings painted on them to denote their value in the game. Woven mats and pointers were also used.

By far the most widespread form of guessing game is the hand game. It occurred throughout the

GAMING

Indian tribes within the United States currently manage more than one hundred high stakes bingo operations and over sixty casino facilities in twenty-four states. Indian gaming has developed into a six-billion-dollar-a-year business, providing tribes with greater economic security. High stakes bingo and casino operations grew rapidly during the 1980s. This quick growth was made necessary by severe

The advent of casino gambling divided the Mohawk Nation into violent factions and brought state government intervention. Here, in 1990, an employee of Tony's Vegas International Casino on the Akwesasne (St. Regis) Reservation in New York sits idly between slot machines as customers were unable to get through a state trooper roadblock on the highway. Akwesasne straddles the borders of New York, in the United States, and Ontario and Quebec, in Canada.

cuts in federal funding to Indian governmental programs. By 1993, over sixty-three tribes had entered into gaming agreements with individual states to establish high stakes gambling facilities, and the number of new operations is increasing.

In 1988, the federal government enacted the Indian Gaming Regulatory Act (IGRA). This act separates gaming into three classes and allows regulatory jurisdiction over each class among tribal, federal, and state governments. This process of jurisdiction is designed to balance the protective goals of the state and the economic interests of the tribe, thus establishing systems of Indian gaming that are beneficial to both the state and the tribe. The Indian Gaming Regulatory Act also requires that bingo and casino operations be tribally owned and that the revenues must be used for specified tribal activities. This ensures a benefit for the whole tribe and not just for a few people within the tribe. Such benefits include providing tribal members with employment opportunities, health and dental care, housing and educational assistance, and

scholarships. Gaming revenue also enables tribes to supplement tribal programs, to fund legal services and tribal land acquisition projects, and to provide loans for other tribal businesses.

Though gaming provides much-needed revenue toward tribal independence, it is not without its conflicts. For instance, in 1990, on the St. Regis Akwesasne Indian Reservation in upstate New York, violence broke out over the appropriate role gaming should play in the Mohawk tribal government. Gaming was supported by a group called the Warrior Society, but traditionalists and elected officials were opposed to gaming. On the Oneida Reservation, tribal factions also disagreed over the role of gaming on the reservation—a dispute that resulted in the destruction of a bingo hall.

Serious controversies in regard to Indian gaming have also arisen between tribal and state governments. Several states fear that Indian gaming will greatly compromise revenue gained from state lotteries—that Indian gaming will cut into their pie. Some states have devised arguments against

Choctaw Bingo in Durant, Oklahoma, a tribal enterprise, has a seating capacity of two thousand for high stakes bingo players, many of whom travel by bus from as far away as Dallas. Other Oklahoma Choctaw high stakes bingo enterprises are located in Pocola and Idabel and at Arrowhead Resort.

gambling; these arguments have raised concerns about public safety and whether tribal law enforcement is competent enough to protect large numbers of patrons. Some states voice concerns in regard to the threat of organized crime infiltrating tribal gaming, although the U.S. Department of Justice has concluded that organized crime has not as of yet gained any access within Indian gaming. These concerns have resulted in some states' refusal to negotiate with tribes, even though the IGRA requires states to do so. Consequently, some tribes have filed suits in federal court.

The growing development of tribal gaming has created enormous debate, and several amendments to the IGRA have been proposed to limit certain aspects of Indian gaming. But despite the many controversies, gaming continues to provide powerful assurance of tribal economic security.

SEE ALSO:
Indian Gaming Regulatory Act of 1988.

GEIOGAMAH, HANAY (1945–)

Hanay Geiogamah is a Kiowa–Delaware writer, producer, and teacher who has gained international attention as a playwright.

Among his most accomplished plays are *Body Indian*, *Foghorn*, and *Coon Cons Coyote*. Geiogamah served as technical consultant on the feature film *Dark Wind*, with Robert Redford as executive producer. He also codirected and helped produce the Public Broadcasting System's feature on the American Indian Dance Theater as part of the *Great Performances: Dance in America* series, which aired in 1990. He also wrote a teleplay of *The Way to Rainy Mountain*, based on N. Scott Momaday's book.

Geiogamah, who has been honored with many awards, including the William Randolph Hearst National Writing Award and the Charles MacMahon Foundation Scholarship in Journalism, began his career in New York City as artistic director of the Native American Theater Ensemble from 1972 to 1976. In 1980, he earned a degree in theater and drama from Indiana University in Bloomington. While at the university, he worked as a director,

producer, instructor, and organizer for American Indian communications and arts projects.

Geiogamah directed the Native Americans in Arts organization from 1980 to 1982. He has also been artistic director of the Native American Theater Ensemble in Los Angeles and the American Indian Dance Theatre in New York City. From 1984 to 1988, Geiogamah was director of communications and then executive director of the American Indian Registry for the Performing Arts in Los Angeles. He has also conducted tours of the American Indian Dance Theatre in the United States and Europe.

Teaching has remained an important part of Geiogamah's work. He taught in the theater department at the University of California at Los Angeles from 1984 to 1992.

Geiogamah continues his work developing and promoting the Native American Theater Ensemble, the American Indian Registry for Performing Arts, and the American Indian Dance Theatre–Native American Performing Arts Foundation.

SEE ALSO:
American Indian Dance Theatre.

GENERAL ALLOTMENT ACT

The General Allotment Act, or the Dawes Severalty Act, was passed in 1887 and amended in 1891, 1906, and 1910. The intention of the act was to make Indians conform to the patterns of American society by forcing them to own land individually, rather than as a nation.

Traditionally, Indian lands were owned in common by everyone in the tribe for the well-being of the entire nation. In fact, Indians had no concept of individual ownership of land. Senator Henry Dawes, for whom the act is named, reported that the Indians worked together for the common good of the tribe without thinking in terms of individuality. He said they showed no selfishness, and selfishness, he believed, is at the basis of civilization. He believed that by forcing Indians to own individual land, they would begin to conform to the society of the colonizers. He and his supporters also believed that Indians would give up their tribal ways and customs.

This painting depicts the land rush that occurred when Indian lands were opened to non-Native ownership under terms of the General Allotment Act.

Pressure from non-Indians who wanted Indian land was the strongest factor behind the passage of the act. With Indian land allotted to individuals of the tribe, not all the Indian-owned land would be taken by the tribal members. This surplus land could then be opened up for non-Native settlement.

After the Allotment Act was passed, Native people would be allowed to sell their individual parcels of land after a period of twenty-five years. It was the belief at the time that over those twenty-five years, Indians would acquire the management skills to handle the land. But nothing was done to encourage such skills, and almost immediately the land was leased to non-Indians who poured into Indian country.

By the mid-1930s, Indians had lost about ninety million acres (thirty-six million hectares), most-ly through fraudulent land sales. Because the entire concept of individually owned land was foreign to Indian people, many sold their land for a fraction of its value.

Most of the Christian denominations supported the Dawes Act, believing that it would help push Indians toward Christianization. They also encouraged the sale of the land to help push Indians to assimilate into the dominant European-American culture.

The U.S. senators of the Dawes Commission also believed that individual allotment would lead to the assimilation of Indians into the dominant culture. Senator John Logan stated as much to Sitting Bull of the Sioux Nation. "The government feeds and clothes and educates your children now, and desires to teach you to become farmers, and to civilize you, and make you as white men," Logan said.

Most of the Indians were allotted 160 acres (64 hectares) per family, which the government thought could sustain them. Even though there was much resistance to these allotments, most of the Indians were finally forced to accept.

Allotment is now understood to have been one of the greatest disasters ever to befall Indian people. In the view of many Native Americans, it was a powerful weapon used against their culture in a campaign of the U.S. Congress to wage cultural genocide against Indian nations and people. The allotment of Indian land finally ended in 1934 with the passage of the Indian Reorganization Act (Indian New Deal), but only after Indian people had lost most of their land.

SEE ALSO:

Acculturation; Dawes Commission; Indian New Deal (Indian Reorganization Act); Self-determination; Termination Policy.